# IMPROVE YOUR DECLARER PLAY AT NO-TRUMPS

There is a great satisfaction in bringing home the number of tricks you need to make your contract. This is increased when you know that you have adopted the best line of play and it has come off. You feel even better when the contract is in no-trumps, where the play is often more difficult because you do not have the security and protection of a trump suit.

This book is about the strategy of succeeding as declarer when you play no-trumps. The first section deals with the approach you should adopt before you even play a card from dummy. Then follow heaps of practical examples, problems for you to solve, deals that arose in major competitions where the very best players did not always find the right answer. Most importantly, the solutions include the logic behind the right play, the clues to locate the missing cards and ideas on how to induce opposition error when you have no legitimate chance for success.

In this book, Australian expert Ron Klinger shows you how to come out on top more often. Where you might have felt reluctance when playing no-trumps, you will emerge with a new sense of confidence. No-trumps will no longer hold any fears for you.

*Ron Klinger is a leading international bridge teacher and has represented Australia in many world championships from 1976 to 2009. He has written over fifty books, some of which have been translated into Bulgarian, Chinese, Danish, French, Hebrew and Icelandic.*

# IMPROVE YOUR DECLARER PLAY AT NO-TRUMPS

Ron Klinger

**Weidenfeld & Nicolson**
IN ASSOCIATION WITH
PETER CRAWLEY

First published in Great Britain 2009
in association with Peter Crawley
by Weidenfeld & Nicolson
a division of the Orion Publishing Group Ltd
Orion House, 5 Upper St Martin's Lane
London, WC2H 9EA

an Hachette Livre UK Company

A catalogue record for this book is available from the British Library

ISBN: 978 0 297 85835 5

Typeset by Modern Bridge Publications
P.O. Box 140, Northbridge NSW 1560, Australia

Printed in Great Britain by Clays Ltd, St Ives plc

The Orion Publishing Group's policy is to use papers that are natural, renewable
and recyclable products and made from wood grown in sustainable forests. The
logging and manufacturing processes are expected to conform to the environ-
mental regulations of the country of origin.

www.orionbooks.co.uk

# Contents

# Introduction

The bidding goes:

| West | North | East | South |
|------|-------|------|----------|
| 1NT  | Pass  | 3NT  | All pass |

The opening lead is made and dummy appears:

♠ 9 5 2
♡ 8 6 5
◊ J 10 4 3
♣ 9 8 7

"How can you raise to 3NT with one point?" West screams.

"But you have always said you hate playing 1NT."

There are players who have a morbid fear of no-trumps, whether it is 1NT, 2NT, 3NT, 6NT or any no-trumps. They will try to manoeuvre the auction so that if the contract turns out to be no-trumps, partner will be declarer. This becomes very tricky if both partners have a no-trumps phobia.

The best way to conquer your fear is to attack it. By adopting the approaches recommended here and tackling the problems that follow, you will not only overcome your anxiety, but you will also become more confident and actually look forward to playing no-trump contracts.

The same applies if you do not actually fear no-trumps, but you do have flutters of nervousness when you lack the protection of a trump suit. Even if you have no worries at all about no-trumps, no doubt you are keen to obtain better results.

This book focuses on no-trump contracts at all levels and the problems that arose in recent international tournaments or national championships. It may be of some comfort to you that some players at this level did not always find the right solution. Your confidence will steadily grow when you find the right play that was perhaps missed at the table.

Study the section on 'Plan Your Play' and aim to adopt the recommended approach. If necessary, read it a second time. Not every aspect is vital for each deal, but you still need to apply those methods when you start each problem and at the table. Make a firm decision about what you would do before consulting the complete deal and the suggested solution. Assume that all the problems are set at teams or rubber bridge. You are required to make your contract, difficult enough a lot of the time, and need not worry about overtricks.

The problems in this book differ from those in other books. There are no set themes or common scenarios. All the deals arose at the table in major events and have not been adjusted.

When you have completed the book, you will notice that your performance in no-trump contracts at the table will improve. Your results will take a leap forward and you can take pride in your enhanced skill.

*Happy bridging.*

*Ron Klinger, 2009*

# *Plan Your Play*

You often see bridge problems in books, magazines, newspapers and the last sentence is 'Plan your play'. What exactly do these words mean? How do you go about forming a plan?

A plan consists of a series of steps you should take to ensure success or at least to give you the best chance to make your contract. The recommended approach for no-trumps is

## C – A – T – C – H

**C**ount your tricks, count the high card points.

**A**nalyse the opening lead.

**T**hird hand's play.

**C**onsider the bidding.

**H**atch your plan.

So, Catch and Hatch.

### Counting

**Count your tricks.** At no-trumps the first thing to do is count the number of instant winners you have. If you have enough for your contract, can you see any problems in taking those tricks? Are any of the suits blocked? In which order should you take the tricks? Is it safe to look for overtricks?

If you are short of the tricks needed for the contract, how many short are you? Where can you find the extra tricks? What is the best way to make them? Is there a danger you must avoid?

Here is a simple example:

♠ J 9 7                 ♠ A 4 2
♡ A 4                  ♡ Q J
♢ 7 6 2                ♢ A J 4 3
♣ A K Q 4 3         ♣ 9 8 6 2

Your methods have brought you to 3NT by West. There has been
no opposition bidding. North leads the ♡10: queen – king – ace.
How should you proceed? Be specific.

**Count your instant winners.** You have one spade, two hearts,
one diamond and three clubs. Total: seven. Two tricks short.
Where will you find two more tricks? From the clubs. As long as
clubs are 2-2 or 3-1 there will be more tricks there. Now the most
important question for this deal: Is there a danger you must avoid?

One moment of carelessness and 3NT might go off. It is vital that
you spot the problem in time. A good declarer will see the risk
and take the appropriate countermeasures. A lesser declarer will
recognise the problem a second or two too late. The 'Oops' factor.

After you take the ♡A, cash the clubs from the top, but make sure
you unblock the nine, eight and six from dummy under the ace,
king and queen. That leaves dummy with the ♣2 and your ♣4,
♣3 will take two more tricks.

If you have played the ♣2 under one of your top clubs and it turns
out the clubs divide 3-1, then after the ♣A, ♣K, ♣Q, dummy's
remaining club will be higher than your ♣4, ♣3. That means the
next club trick will be won in dummy and with no re-entry to your
hand, you will make only eight tricks. The solution is easy, but
you have to spot it in time.

**Count the high card points.** As soon as dummy appears, count the high card points in dummy and add your own. Take the total from forty and that gives you the number of HCP held by the opponents. If either opponent has bid, you might easily be able to place the location of the missing high cards. For a working approach, assume an opening bidder has about 12 HCP or more, a responder who passed partner's opening has 0-5, and an overcaller has about 9+ HCP. These will not always be 100% accurate, but they are a reasonable basis.

Here is an easy exercise:

Dealer North : North-South vulnerable

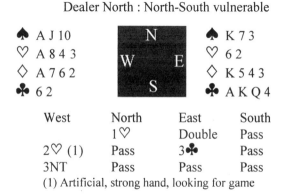

| | ♠ A J 10 | | ♠ K 7 3 |
| | ♡ A 8 4 3 | | ♡ 6 2 |
| | ◇ A 7 6 2 | | ◇ K 5 4 3 |
| | ♣ 6 2 | | ♣ A K Q 4 |

| West | North | East | South |
|------|-------|------|-------|
| | 1 ♡ | Double | Pass |
| 2♡ (1) | Pass | 3♣ | Pass |
| 3NT | Pass | Pass | Pass |

(1) Artificial, strong hand, looking for game

North leads the ♡K. Plan your play. If you duck, North continues with top hearts.

**Count your tricks.** You have eight instant winners. Where will you find your ninth trick? From diamonds if they are 3-2 or from a successful spade finesse. Is there any danger? If you play on diamonds and North has the third diamond, you will fail.

**Count the points.** Dummy has 15, you have 13. Total: 28. Points missing: 12. North opened the bidding. Play the ♠A and lead the ♠J, playing North to hold the ♠Q. Almost a sure thing.

**Analyse the opening lead.** The opening lead can provide lots of useful information. Be aware of your opponents' methods. Do they lead fourth-highest? Then th e lead of a two signifies at most a 4-card suit and you can deduce the how many cards are held by third hand in that suit. Do they lead thirds-and-fifths? Now the lead of a two shows three or five cards in the suit. Most of the time the opening leader will have five. Again you can work out the layout of the suit.

What about attitude leads? With this method the player leads the lowest available card to show great interest in the suit led, a middling card to show moderate interest and a high spot card to show very little interest. This can help you assess the high card location within that suit.

Is the opening lead an honour card? Again, what are their methods? Most lead top-of-sequence, but some 'underlead' (second-highest card from a sequence). You must be aware of this.

Some lead 'strong tens', meaning that the lead of a ten indicates an interior sequence, while the lead of a jack or a nine denies an interior sequence. Suppose you have this position:

North
♠ Q 6 5

West leads the ♠10

South
♠ A 7 2

Playing 'strong tens' West's spades should be headed by the K-J-10. You can play the queen and expect it to win. What if West, playing strong tens, had led the ♠J? Now you can deduce that West does not have the ♠K. Play low from dummy and take the ♠A. If West regains the lead and plays the ♠10, play low from dummy again. Maybe East began with ♠K doubleton.

Try this problem:

| ♠ A 5 3 | | ♠ 8 4 |
|---------|--------|-------|
| ♡ K 4 3 | **N** | ♡ A Q J 6 |
| ◇ K Q 10 7 | **W    E** | ◇ J 9 5 |
| ♣ 10 9 2 | **S** | ♣ A Q J 7 |

You have reached 3NT by West and North leads the ♠2. Plan your play.

**Count tricks:** You have six. Tricks needed: three. Where can you find them? Either from the diamonds by knocking out the ace or by finessing in clubs. Which should you choose?

**Analyse the lead:** If the lead is fourth-highest, spades figure to be 4-4. You should take the ♠A and knock out the ◇A. If you take the club finesse and it loses, you will lose three spades, a diamond and a club.

If they are leading thirds-and-fifths, you can expect North to have five spades. You should hold off until the third round of spades. Then take the club finesse. You succeed if North has the king. Even if the club finesse loses, you make 3NT if South has the ◇A, as South should be out of spades.

If you judge North began with five spades, it would be unwise to hold off in spades and then play a diamond. You would fail if North has the ◇A, while if North also has the ♣K, you could have made your contract. If North has five spades and the ◇A and South has the ♣K, 3NT was doomed.

You are entitled to notice how long the opening lead takes. Strong players almost always make the opening lead at the same pace. They have been working on their opening lead during the auction and usually need little further time.

Luckily not all your opponents are experts. Against no-trumps a good lead is obvious and will appear quickly. If the lead takes some time, you can assume that the player on lead does not have an obviously good lead. If the lead turns out to be highly unusual, as from a short suit, try to deduce why that lead was chosen.

**Third hand's play.** More evidence is available from the card played by third hand. If the opening lead was low and dummy has played a low card, third hand plays high. If it is an honour card, standard play is to follow with the cheapest of equally high cards. That means the honour card played as third-hand-high denies the next cheaper honour.

Apply that to this problem:

Dealer North : Both vulnerable

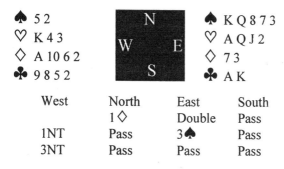

| ♠ 5 2 | | | |
| ♡ K 4 3 | | | |
| ◇ A 10 6 2 | | | |
| ♣ 9 8 5 2 | | | |

| ♠ K Q 8 7 3 |
| ♡ A Q J 2 |
| ◇ 7 3 |
| ♣ A K |

| West | North | East | South |
|------|-------|------|-------|
|      | 1 ◇   | Double | Pass |
| 1NT  | Pass  | 3 ♠  | Pass  |
| 3NT  | Pass  | Pass | Pass  |

West leads the ◇ 5 (fourth-highest): three – queen . . .
Plan your play.

**Count tricks:** Seven. The two extra need to come from the spades.

**Count HCP:** Dummy has 19, you have 7. Total: 26. Missing: 14.

**Analyse the lead:** Fourth-highest. North has four or five diamonds (as you can see the two and the three).

**Third hand's play:** The ◇Q denies the ◇J. With the ◇Q gone, only 12 HCP are missing. As North opened the bidding, North figures to have all of the missing high cards. It is vital you take the ◇A at trick 1 and lead a spade at once as you know North has the ♠A. If North ducks, win with dummy's king and return to hand via the ♡K to lead another spade. North can take the ♠A and if North cashes the ◇K, ◇J, your ◇10 becomes high.

The danger is to duck the opening lead. If South began with ◇Q-8 and you duck the ◇Q, South returns the ◇8. If you duck again, North can over-take with the ◇9 from an original holding of ◇K-J-9-5-4 and knock out your ◇A. Now you will lose four diamonds and the ♠A. By counting the points and noting the play by third hand, you knew it was safe to take the ◇A at trick one, as your remaining ◇10-6-2 would be a stopper against North.

**Consider the bidding.** You might have done this already when you counted the points, but it will not hurt to check the auction again. Their bidding can give you an idea of the strength of the opposing hands and their shape, especially if an opponent has bid two suits or made a takeout double. Where a player opened with a pre-empt and has shown up with a strong suit, most of the missing strength will be with the other opponent. After the first trick or two, as more cards are revealed, you will be able to place the missing cards more accurately.

Sometimes you have no immediate information as both opponents passed throughout. Even so, you may be able to glean information from a player who has passed. Did an opponent fail to open the bidding, yet turn up with 10 HCP already? You can assume all the other missing high cards are with the other opponent. Did an opponent pass as dealer, but make a takeout double or an overcall later? It is likely that the player has just below opening values, about 9-11 HCP. Did an opponent fail to reply to an opening bid or an overcall? That also limits the possible values.

**Hatch your plan.** This includes decisions such as whether to win the opening lead or whether to hold up, in which hand to take the first trick when there is a choice or which suit to tackle next. If you have done your homework on the first four items in your checklist, then your plan should virtually be hatched already. Remember, you will use this approach every time you are declarer at no-trumps:

**Count** your tricks, **count** the high card points.

**Analyse** the opening lead.

**Third** hand's play.

**Consider** the bidding.

**Hatch** your plan.

Now let's start on the problems . . .

Unlike most books with play problems, there are no esoteric deals or special themes, just practical problems, which arose at the table in world competition or major national events in recent years. The good news is that you will probably do better, and certainly not worse, than quite a few of the players who actually faced these problems.

After you have been through all the problems once, it is not a bad idea to tackle them again, perhaps in a year's time. Practice may not make perfect, but it will certainly make you better.

# *Test Your Play*

**1.** Dealer East : Nil vulnerable

| | West | North | East | South |
|---|---|---|---|---|
| ♠ K J 2 | | | Pass | 1♣ |
| ♡ K Q J 10 9 4 | | | | |
| ◇ Q | Pass | 1♡ | Pass | 1♠ |
| ♣ 8 6 4 | Pass | 3♡ | Pass | 3NT |
| | Pass | Pass | Pass | |

| |
|---|
| ♠ Q 7 4 3 |
| ♡ A |
| ◇ K 4 3 2 |
| ♣ K J 5 3 |

The 1♣ opening was dictated by system. West leads the ◇J and dummy's ◇Q wins.

Plan your play.

*Solution on page 18.*

**2.** Dealer North : Both vulnerable

| | West | North | East | South |
|---|---|---|---|---|
| ♠ A 3 2 | | 1♣ | 1♠ | 2◇ |
| ♡ J 7 | | | | |
| ◇ A 10 9 | Pass | 3◇ | Pass | 3NT |
| ♣ K J 10 8 5 | Pass | Pass | Pass | |

| |
|---|
| ♠ Q 8 6 |
| ♡ Q 8 3 |
| ◇ K J 7 6 4 |
| ♣ A 7 |

West leads the ♠10.

Plan your play.

*Solution on page 19.*

**1.**    Dealer East : Nil vulnerable

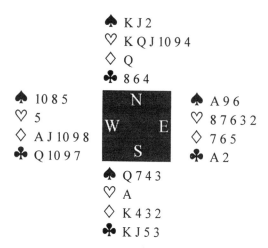

&spades; K J 2
&hearts; K Q J 10 9 4
&diams; Q
&clubs; 8 6 4

&spades; 10 8 5
&hearts; 5
&diams; A J 10 9 8
&clubs; Q 10 9 7

&spades; A 9 6
&hearts; 8 7 6 3 2
&diams; 7 6 5
&clubs; A 2

&spades; Q 7 4 3
&hearts; A
&diams; K 4 3 2
&clubs; K J 5 3

From a National Open Teams event, 2008: South is in 3NT with no opposition bidding and West leads the &diams;J. You have one diamond trick when the &diams;Q wins and six tricks available in hearts. As the hearts are blocked your first task is to play a heart to your ace to clear the blockage.

You need two more tricks and the best hope is via the spade suit. At trick 3 you lead a low spade and West follows low. Which spade honour do you play from dummy?

It seems as though it makes no difference, but the right card is the &spades;K. East takes it with the &spades;A and returns a diamond. You play low and West is forced to win. If West plays a club next, you will fail when East wins and returns a diamond, but at the table West played another spade and South had ten tricks. Had you played the &spades;J from dummy, West would know another spade was futile.

Quite a few made 3NT, but perhaps some Souths opened 1&diams; and might have escaped a diamond lead. After the &clubs;10 lead to the ace and the &clubs;2 back, South takes the &clubs;K and is safe.

**2.**  Dealer North : Both vulnerable

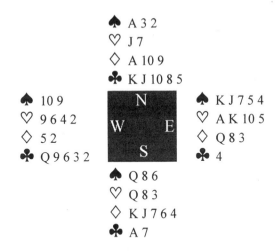

♠ A 3 2
♡ J 7
◇ A 10 9
♣ K J 10 8 5

♠ 10 9
♡ 9 6 4 2
◇ 5 2
♣ Q 9 6 3 2

♠ K J 7 5 4
♡ A K 10 5
◇ Q 8 3
♣ 4

♠ Q 8 6
♡ Q 8 3
◇ K J 7 6 4
♣ A 7

From a National Butler Trials, 2008: South is in 3NT after East overcalled 1♠. West leads the ♠10. You have five tricks on top and need four more. These can come from one or both minors. You have 25 HCP. East will have most of the other 15.

What do you make of the ♠10 lead? That figures to be a singleton or top from a doubleton. That places the ♠K with East. Is there a danger if you play low from dummy? East will win and might shift to hearts where you have only one stopper. Then if you misguess in a minor suit, the defence can take that minor suit queen, one spade and three hearts.

Take the ♠A at once and start on the minors. Now if you misguess one minor, you still succeed if you pick the other.

Most declarers in 3NT succeeded. One failed by ducking the ♠10 lead. East switched to ♡A, ♡K and a third heart. South played ◇A, ◇K, ♣A, club to the jack and was one down. Win the ♠A at trick 1 and you can finesse in both minors.

**3.** Dealer South : East-West vulnerable

| ♠ A K Q 9 5 | West | North | East | South |
|---|---|---|---|---|
| ♡ A J 8 | | | | 1♣ |
| ♢ J 10 6 | Pass | 1♡ (1) | Pass | 1NT (2) |
| ♣ J 8 | Pass | 3NT | All pass | |

| N |
|---|
| W          E |
| S |

(1) Shows 4+ spades   (2) Denies three spades

West leads the ♡ 3 (thirds-and-fifths):
jack – king – nine. East returns the ♡ 6.

♠ 4
♡ Q 10 9          Plan your play.
♢ Q 9 3 2
♣ A Q 6 4 3      *Solution opposite .*

*Checklist*

**Count Tricks:** After trick 1 South has six tricks (three spades, two hearts and one club). Three tricks are needed.

**Count HCP:** North has 16, South has 10. Total: 26. There is no evidence as to the likely location of the missing points.

**Analyse the lead:** Playing thirds-and-fifths the ♡3 can be bottom of three or third from four. It cannot be from a 5-card suit. East returned the ♡6. The ♡2 is missing. If West had started with five hearts, West would have led the ♡2.

**Third-hand play:** Routine. No significance there.

**Consider the bidding:** None relevant.

**Hatch your plan:** Where do you win trick 2? What do you play at trick 3?

The deal arose in the semi-finals of the 2008 Asian Cup:

Dealer South : East-West vulnerable

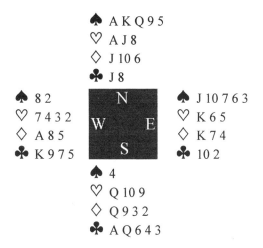

♠ A K Q 9 5
♡ A J 8
◇ J 10 6
♣ J 8

♠ 8 2                    ♠ J 10 7 6 3
♡ 7 4 3 2               ♡ K 6 5
◇ A 8 5                  ◇ K 7 4
♣ K 9 7 5               ♣ 10 2

♠ 4
♡ Q 10 9
◇ Q 9 3 2
♣ A Q 6 4 3

Over the four divisions (Open, Women's, Seniors, Youth) 3NT was played 14 times and made eight times.

In the Open, one declarer won trick two with the ♡A, and led the ◇J. East took the ◇K and played another heart. West won the next diamond and cashed the thirteenth heart. When the club finesse lost, South was one down.

It is better to win trick 2 with the ♡A and lead the ♣J. If it loses, perhaps clubs are 3-3. If it is covered, you win and start on diamonds. It is unlikely they will win and attack your clubs.

Another benefit of leading the ♣J at trick 3 occurred at one of the other tables. West ducked the jack smoothly and now declarer switched to diamonds and made nine tricks in comfort.

**4.** Dealer North : Nil vulnerable

| | ♠ K 4 3 2 | West | North | East | South |
|---|---|---|---|---|---|
| | ♡ A K Q 5 4 | | 1♡ | Pass | 2♣ |
| | ♢ Q 8 3 2 | Pass | 2♠ | Pass | 3NT |
| | ♣ - - - | Pass | Pass | Pass | |

```
        N
   W         E
        S
```

♠ J 10 5
♡ 2
♢ J 10 6 5
♣ A K J 6 4

South's 2♣ was artificial, 10-12 points. West leads the ♣9. You pitch the ♡4 from dummy, East plays the ♣2* and you win with the ♣J.
*Low-encouraging
Plan your play.

*Solution opposite .*

*Checklist*

**Count Tricks:** After trick 1 South has six tricks (three hearts and three clubs). Three tricks are needed.

**Count HCP:** North has 14, South has 10. Total: 24. There is no evidence as to the likely location of the missing points.

**Analyse the lead:** With standard leads, the ♣9 cannot be a genuine fourth-highest or middle-up-down. Against no-trumps, players often use top-of-nothing.

**Third-hand play:** East's signal with the ♣2 shows interest in clubs (low-like). You can place East with the ♣Q and ♣10. This confirms that West has led top from a worthless holding.

**Consider the bidding:** None relevant.

**Hatch your plan:** What will you play at trick 2?

The deal is Board 11, Round 7 of the 2008 World Open Teams:

Dealer North : Nil vulnerable

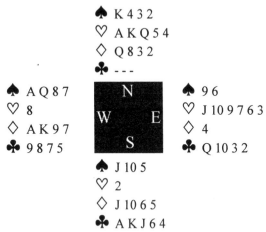

The bidding was not pretty, but because the 2♣ response was artificial, West began with the ♣9 (top-of-nothing and akin to an attitude lead: high card = no interest).

In similar vein to the recommended play in Problem #3, South led the ♠J at trick 2. South hoped that the opponents think South was trying to set up spade tricks and might duck the ♠J. If so, he could then start on diamonds.

West won with the ♠A and played another club. South won and led a low diamond. West took the ◇K and played a third club. South won and played another diamond. West won and played a club, but South had the rest. The defence could have done better, but note South's idea of trying to steal a spade trick early.

3NT was bid and made 8/12 times in the Open Teams, 7/11 in the Women's and 4/5 in the Seniors.

**5.** Dealer South : Nil vulnerable

♠ A 8 7 5 4
♡ A K 9
♢ J 7 4
♣ 7 2

| West | North | East | South |
|------|-------|------|-------|
|      |       |      | Pass |
| Pass | 1♠ | Pass | 1NT |
| Pass | Pass | Dble (1) | All pass |

(1) Double is for takeout of spades

West leads the ♡3, thirds-and-fifths.

♠ 9 2
♡ 10 8 4
♢ A 10 3
♣ A 8 6 5 3

Plan your play.

*Solution opposite.*

*Checklist*

**Count Tricks:** South has five tricks. Two tricks are needed.

**Count HCP:** North has 12, South has 8. Total: 20.

**Analyse the lead:** Playing thirds-and-fifths the ♡3 can be bottom of three or five, or third from four. As East made a belated takeout double of spades, East will have some length in hearts and so the ♡ 3 figures to be from three or four cards.

**Third-hand play:** Not relevant yet.

**Consider the bidding:** East failed to double 1♠ for takeout, but made a balancing double later. That suggests East has 9-11 points and so the missing 20 points will be split about evenly. West's pass of the double indicates values in spades.

**Hatch your plan:** Do you take this trick or duck it? Where will you find two more tricks?

This was Board 11, Round 15 of the 2008 World Open Teams:

Dealer South : Nil vulnerable

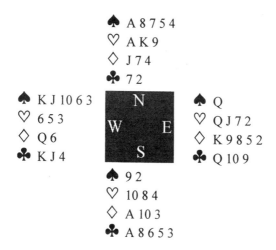

In the Open Teams, 1NT was reached 39 times and made only 26 times. Some made eight tricks, some made five. In the Women's, 1NT succeeded 26/37 times. It was not played in the Seniors.

The two extra tricks you need will not come from spades. East's takeout double indicates shortage in spades. Do not expect a 3-3 split there. You might score one extra trick in diamonds, but your best hope is to find clubs 3-3.

Take the first heart with the ace (the chance of West holding both ♡Q and ♡J is remote) and duck a club. When you regain the lead, play the ♣A and another club. On a lucky day you have your seven tricks.

If East wins the first club and plays a low diamond, ducked to West's ◇Q, make sure you play the ◇J from dummy if West returns a diamond. That preserves an entry to your hand.

**6.** Dealer North : East-West vulnerable

♠ Q J
♡ A K 10 9 3
♢ 6 4
♣ J 7 5 2

| West | North | East | South |
|------|-------|------|-------|
|      | 1♡    | Pass | 1♠    |
| 2♢   | Pass  | Pass | 3NT   |
| Pass | Pass  | Pass |       |

West leads the ♢Q.

Plan your play.

♠ K 8 7 4 2
♡ 7
♢ A K 2
♣ A 10 6 3

*Solution opposite.*

*Checklist*

**Count Tricks:** South has five tricks. Four tricks are needed.

**Count HCP:** North has 11, South has 14. Total: 25. Most of the missing 15 HCP will be with West for the vulnerable overcall.

**Analyse the lead:** West's ♢Q means the diamonds will be headed by ♢Q-J-10 or ♢Q-J-9.

**Third-hand play:** Not relevant yet.

**Consider the bidding:** West has made a 2♢ overcall, vulnerable against not, with a suit headed by the queen. You can expect West to have significant values outside diamonds.

**Hatch your plan:** Do you take this trick or duck it? Where will you find four more tricks?

The deal arose in a National Open Teams event, 2008:

Dealer North : East-West vulnerable

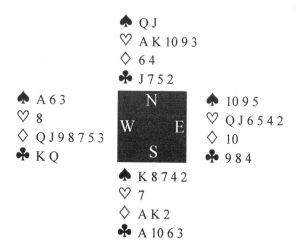

♠ Q J
♡ A K 10 9 3
◇ 6 4
♣ J 7 5 2

♠ A 6 3
♡ 8
◇ Q J 9 8 7 5 3
♣ K Q

♠ 10 9 5
♡ Q J 6 5 4 2
◇ 10
♣ 9 8 4

♠ K 8 7 4 2
♡ 7
◇ A K 2
♣ A 10 6 3

Needing four more tricks, the best hope by far is to find spades 3-3. Take the first diamond and play the ♠Q. If it wins, play the ♠J. If that also wins, cross to the ♣A and play another spade. If spades are 3-3, you are home. As it happens, after the ♣A drops an honour, it is easier still.

A top player went off after ducking the opening lead. West played a second diamond. South won and played ♠Q, ♠J, which held. Declarer could still have succeeded via a club to the ace since the lucky club position will give declarer two more tricks there.

Instead, South ran the ♣J to West's king. South won the diamond return and could not afford another spade, else West would cash the rest of the diamonds. After playing off the ♡K, ♡A, South played a club to the ten and now went three down. 3NT made 16 times out of 18.

**7.** Dealer West : North-South vulnerable

| West | North | East | South |
|------|-------|------|-------|
|      |       | Pass | 1◇ | Pass | 1♠ |

♠ 10
♡ 10 8 5 2
◇ A K 9 4
♣ A K J 7

| | | Pass | 2♣ | Pass | 3◇ |
| | | Pass | 3♡ | Pass | 3NT |
| | | Pass | Pass | Pass |

3♡ sought help in hearts for no-trumps.
West leads the ♡3 (fourth-highest). East wins
with the ♡A and returns the ♡7: queen –
king – five. West switches to the ♣5.

♠ A Q J 6
♡ Q 6
◇ Q 10 3 2
♣ 10 9 2

Plan your play.

*Solution opposite .*

*Checklist*

**Count Tricks:** South has six tricks. Three tricks are needed.

**Count HCP:** North has 15, South has 11. Total: 25. The only
evidence is that West is a passed hand.

**Analyse the lead:** West's heart lead, the 'unbid' suit was normal.
The ♡3 can be from a 4-card suit (not five, as the ♡2 is in dummy)
or possibly from ♡K-x-3.

**Third-hand play:** East's return of the ♡7 could be from A-J-9-7,
but then West would have played a third heart. West's shift at
trick 3 indicates West has some critical holding in hearts, perhaps
♡K-J-x-3 or ♡K-J-3 or ♡K-9-3.

**Consider the bidding:** None relevant.

**Hatch your plan:** If the diamonds behave, you have an extra trick
there. Will you try the spades or take the club finesse?

The deal comes from the semi-finals of a National Open Teams event in 2008:

Dealer West : North-South vulnerable

♠ 10
♡ 10 8 5 2
◇ A K 9 4
♣ A K J 7

♠ K 9 8 3
♡ K J 9 3
◇ J 6
♣ 8 5 4

♠ 7 5 4 2
♡ A 7 4
◇ 8 7 5
♣ Q 6 3

♠ A Q J 6
♡ Q 6
◇ Q 10 3 2
♣ 10 9 2

Three North-South pairs played 3NT and all were successful. West led the ♡3 to the ace, captured the ♡Q on East's ♡7 return and shifted to the ♣5. Should South finesse the ♣J?

Chances for an extra trick in diamonds are excellent and that leaves two more to find. If the club finesse works, you have two extra tricks, but what if it fails? Now you need an extra trick from spades. If the ♣Q and the ♠K are both wrong, you are one off if you take the club finesse.

In fact you need only the two top tricks from the clubs. Take the ♣A, cash the ◇A, ◇K. When they break, lead the ♠10 and let it run. If it holds, cross to the ◇Q and play ♠A, ♠Q. You make three spades, four diamonds and two clubs. Once the heart suit is safe from attack, the club finesse is a red herring.

**8.** Dealer West : Both vulnerable

|  | West | North | East | South |
|---|---|---|---|---|
| ♠ A K Q 2 | Pass | 1♣ | Pass | 1◊ |
| ♡ J 2 | Pass | 1♠ | Pass | 1NT |
| ◊ K 8 | Pass | 2NT | Pass | 3NT |
| ♣ Q J 7 6 4 | Pass | Pass | Pass | |

|   |
|---|
| N |
| W        E |
| S |

♠ 10 9 3
♡ K 10 8 4
◊ Q J 4 2
♣ A 2

West leads the ♡9: jack, ace. East shifts to the ◊10: two – three – king. You run the ♣Q to West's king and West returns the ♣3 to the ace, East discarding the ♠5.

Plan your play.

*Solution opposite.*

*Checklist*

**Count Tricks:** After trick 4 South has seven tricks (three spades, one heart, one diamond and two clubs). Two more tricks are needed.

**Count HCP:** North has 16, South has 10. Total: 26. The only evidence is that West is a passed hand.

**Analyse the lead:** West's ♡9 lead looks to be top-of-nothing. If so, the ♡Q will be with East.

**Third-hand play:** East's shift to the ◊10 suggests a sequence holding, but the ◊A figures to be with West, else East would not lead the suit, but rather wait to capture dummy's king.

**Consider the bidding:** None relevant.

**Hatch your plan:** You can set up one extra trick in diamonds and the heart finesse can be your ninth trick. Is there anything better?

The deal occurred in the 2008 European Open Teams:

Dealer West : Both vulnerable

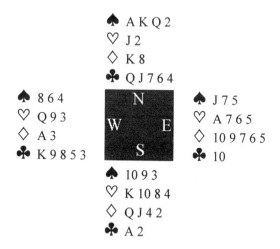

```
              ♠ A K Q 2
              ♡ J 2
              ◇ K 8
              ♣ Q J 7 6 4
  ♠ 8 6 4                        ♠ J 7 5
  ♡ Q 9 3          N            ♡ A 7 6 5
  ◇ A 3        W       E        ◇ 10 9 7 6 5
  ♣ K 9 8 5 3      S            ♣ 10
              ♠ 10 9 3
              ♡ K 10 8 4
              ◇ Q J 4 2
              ♣ A 2
```

Against 3NT West led the ♡9, a deceptive negative-attitude lead, suggesting top-of-nothing.

With seven tricks available South played the ◇Q at trick 5. West won with the ◇A and continued with the ♣9 to North's ♣J. East discarded the ♠7. South should now test the spades. When they behave, declarer has nine tricks via four spades, a heart, two diamonds and two clubs. Playing teams, South should simply cash the tricks and make the contract.

In practice, when declarer cashed the ♠A, the ♠J fell. Seeing the prospect of an easy overtrick, he crossed to the ♠10, cashed the ◇J and returned to the spades. On the last spade West pitched the ♡3. North had the ♡2, ♣7, South had the ♡K-10 and West the ♡Q, ♣8. When declarer finessed the ♡10 for an overtrick the contract was one down. There is a message here for all of us.

**9.** Dealer North : Both vulnerable

| | | | |
|---|---|---|---|
| ♠ Q 9 8 7 3 | West | North | East | South |
| ♡ A Q 7 | | 1♠ | Pass | 2NT (1) |
| ♢ 10 5 2 | Pass | 3NT | All pass | |
| ♣ A 10 | | (1) 13-15 points, balanced, forcing to game | | |

Playing top of sequence, West leads the ♢Q.
East plays the ♢8, high-discouraging.

♠ A J 4
♡ K 9 4 2    Plan your play.
♢ A 7 3
♣ Q 6 5    *Solution opposite.*

*Checklist*

**Count Tricks:** South has six tricks. Three more are needed.

**Count HCP:** North has 12, South has 14. Total: 26. Other than the lead, there is no evidence about the missing points.

**Analyse the lead:** Unless West is doing something strange, the ♢Q lead figures to be from a suit headed by Q-J-9. It would be unusual for West to be leading a doubleton after this auction.

**Third-hand play:** With ♢K-x, East would unblock the king and so you can deduce that East does not have this holding. East's ♢8 looks to be a discouraging signal.

**Consider the bidding:** None relevant.

**Hatch your plan:** Make up your mind how you will play before consulting the full deal.

The deal arose in the final of the 2008 Asian Cup:

Dealer North : Both vulnerable

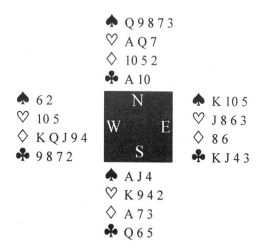

```
              ♠ Q 9 8 7 3
              ♡ A Q 7
              ◇ 10 5 2
              ♣ A 10
♠ 6 2                        ♠ K 10 5
♡ 10 5           N          ♡ J 8 6 3
◇ K Q J 9 4   W     E       ◇ 8 6
♣ 9 8 7 2        S          ♣ K J 4 3
              ♠ A J 4
              ♡ K 9 4 2
              ◇ A 7 3
              ♣ Q 6 5
```

On a normal day West leads the ◇K and South ducks. South takes the second diamond or third diamond, sets up the spades and makes at least nine tricks. To guard against West's having the bare ♠K as the entry to the diamonds, South can start the spades by cashing the ♠A.

In practice, because he had no outside entry West began with a deceptive ◇Q. If East had the ◇A, West expected East to take the ace and return the suit. If declarer had the ◇A, perhaps he would misread the position. That is precisely what happened. Thinking East had at least ◇K-x-x, South took the ◇A at trick 1 and when East came in with the ♠K, he returned a diamond. One down. At the other table declarer made ten tricks in 3NT, +630, +12 Imps.

South should duck the ◇Q anyway. South's fear, that West shifts to a club to East's king and East reverts to diamonds, is a remote chance. As with Problem 8, in this dog-eat-dog world these days, it pays not to trust the opponents too much.

**10.** Dealer North : East-West vulnerable

♠ K Q 7 5 4 2
♡ K
◇ 8 6 5 4
♣ J 4

♠ J 9 6 3
♡ A 6
◇ A K 10 7
♣ A Q 2

North opened a multi-2◇ and, in reply to South's queries, showed a good weak two in spades, a control in hearts, one key card plus the ♠Q. En route South had shown a control in clubs and after learning of the ♠Q, South jumped to 6♠. West doubled and South ran to 6NT, doubled by East.

West leads the ♣3 and the ♣J wins. South plays on spades. West takes the ♠A on the third round, East discarding ♡2, ◇2, ♡3. West exits with the ♡4, East following. Plan your play.
*Solution opposite.*

*Checklist*

**Count Tricks:** After trick 4, South has eleven tricks (five spades, two hearts, two diamonds and two clubs). One more is needed.

**Count HCP:** North has 9, South has 18. Total: 27. The evidence about the missing points is what you have seen so far and the two doubles, one by each opponent.

**Analyse the lead:** With the ♣J winning trick 1, the ♣K figures to be with West. With dummy known to have long spades, it appears that West opted for an attacking lead.

**Third-hand play:** East's discards are all primarily discouraging.

**Consider the bidding:** You should work out what is going on by focussing on the two doubles.

**Hatch your plan:** How do you hope to find the twelfth trick?

From the 2008 European Open Teams:

Dealer North : East-West vulnerable

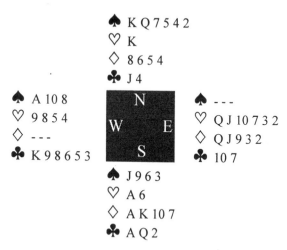

After a multi-2♦ by North, South later bid 6♠ to be played by North and West doubled. South ran to 6NT, which was doubled by East. West led the ♣3 (a heart looks more attractive, but 6NT can be made on any lead) and dummy's ♣J won. After dislodging the ♠A, South had eleven tricks and needed to find the twelfth.

South must ask why West doubled 6♠. Yes, West has the ♠A, but West cannot be sure of any other trick. The double by the player not on lead against a slam usually asks for an unusual lead and often heralds a void. South should read West for a diamond void and play a diamond to the ten for the twelfth trick. At the table declarer played a diamond to the king and was one down.

West's double was not such a great idea. East might have led a diamond anyway or might have picked West to be void in *hearts*. Had West led a heart and South picks the diamond void, South can score four diamond tricks because of the excellent diamond spots.

**11.** Dealer West : North-South vulnerable

♠ K Q
♡ Q 8 7
◇ K 8 6 2
♣ Q J 7 6

| | West | North | East | South |
|---|---|---|---|---|
| | 1♠ | Pass | Pass | 1NT (1) |
| | Pass | 3NT | All pass | |

(1) 11-14, balanced

♠ J 8 2
♡ K J 9 3
◇ A Q 7
♣ K 10 3

It is attractive to have a stopper in their suit for a balancing 1NT, but it is not always possible. South judged that a re-opening 1NT was a better description than a takeout double.

West leads the ♣4 (fourth-highest). The ♠K wins in dummy. East plays the ♠10.

Plan your play.

*Solution opposite .*

*Checklist*

**Count Tricks:** After trick 1, South has four tricks (one spade and three diamonds). Five more are needed.

**Count HCP:** North has 13, South has 14. Total: 27. Almost all of the missing points should be with West for the 1♠ opening.

**Analyse the lead:** The ♣4 as fourth-highest means West began with a 5-card suit (or four if that is available in their methods). As you have the ♠2, West cannot have six spades.

**Third-hand play:** East's ♠10 signal tells West you have the ♠J.

**Consider the bidding:** West's 1♠ opening and East's pass locate the three missing aces for you.

**Hatch your plan:** How do you hope to find nine tricks before West can collect five?

The deal arose in a national teams event in 2008:

Dealer West : North-South vulnerable

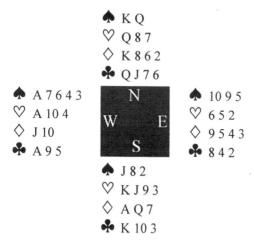

Against 3NT West led the ♠4, won in dummy. You have four top tricks. You can set up plenty of winners, but West can come to three spade tricks and two red aces before you can reach nine tricks. You and dummy have 27 HCP and so West is sure to have the three missing aces for the opening bid.

If diamonds are 3-3, you will have an extra diamond trick and need set up three tricks in only one of the other suits, but what if diamonds are not 3-3? Your best hope then is to have West play second-hand low on hearts or clubs. With the hearts weaker in dummy, that is the better prospect.

Come to hand with a diamond and lead a low heart. West should rise with ♡A and clear the spades, but West might duck in the hope of East having ♡J-x-x. Once the ♡Q wins, switch to clubs to create three tricks there and you will be fine. A top class defender will not fall for your trap, but top class defenders are rare opponents. Eights pairs tried 3NT. Three were successful.

**12.** Dealer South : Nil vulnerable

| | | | | |
|---|---|---|---|---|
| ♠ 10 4 | West | North | East | South |
| ♡ Q 8 6 2 | | | | 1NT (1) |
| ◇ 10 8 5 | Pass | Pass | Pass | |
| ♣ K 7 6 2 | (1) 15-17 | | | |

West leads the ♠Q: four – five – king.
East-West play low-encouraging.

♠ K 9 2          Plan your play.
♡ A J 10 3
◇ K 4            *Solution opposite.*
♣ A J 10 5

*Checklist*

**Count Tricks:** After trick 1, South has four tricks (one spade, one heart and two clubs). Three more are needed.

**Count HCP:** North has 5, South has 16. Total: 21. The absence of a penalty double means neither opponent has a huge hand.

**Analyse the lead:** The ♠Q suggests West has led from ♠Q-J-x or from ♠A-Q-J-x(-x-x). As the ♠9 and the ♠10 are visible, the lead is not the normal top of a sequence.

**Third-hand play:** East's ♠5 seems to be low-like, encouraging a spade continuation.

**Consider the bidding:** Not applicable, but the lack of a 2♠ bid from West suggests that West does not have ♠A-Q-J-x-x-x.

**Hatch your plan:** The club suit has scope for two extra tricks and the heart suit for three extra. What is your best approach?

The deal comes from a 2008 national teams event:

Dealer South : Nil vulnerable

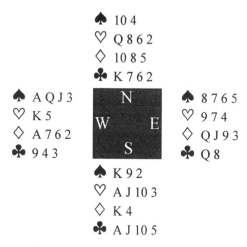

♠ 10 4
♡ Q 8 6 2
◇ 10 8 5
♣ K 7 6 2

♠ A Q J 3          ♠ 8 7 6 5
♡ K 5             ♡ 9 7 4
◇ A 7 6 2         ◇ Q J 9 3
♣ 9 4 3           ♣ Q 8

♠ K 9 2
♡ A J 10 3
◇ K 4
♣ A J 10 5

After the ♠K won trick 1, South had four tricks on top. Three more tricks are available from the hearts if East began with ♡K-x or ♡K-x-x.

You can do better than cross to the ♣K and lead the ♡Q. Instead, play the ♣A, followed by the ♣J. There are some Wests who might cover an honour with an honour. When West plays low, rise with the ♣K. If the ♣Q has not dropped, tackle the hearts.

South did play ♣A and the ♣J to the king. When the ♣Q fell, South had six tricks and cashed the ♣10, followed by the ♣5 to dummy. East discarded a spade on the third club and then a heart. West threw a diamond. East's discard was helpful. It meant East did not start with ♠A-x-x-x-x and so was unlikely to come on lead to push a diamond through the king. The ♡Q lost to the king. West cashed the ♠J and, in a desperate attempt to give East the lead, continued with the ♠3. South won with the ♠9 and wound up with nine tricks. Ten Souths played 1NT. Five were defeated.

**13.** Dealer West : North-South vulnerable

|  | West | North | East | South |
|---|---|---|---|---|
| ♠ 10 8 2 | Pass | Pass | Pass | 1NT (1) |
| ♡ A 9 2 | Pass | 2NT | Pass | 3NT |
| ♢ A J 10 4 | Pass | Pass | Pass | |
| ♣ Q 10 3 | (1) 11+ to 14 points | | | |

|  |  |
|---|---|
| N W E S | This was the actual auction. There are some who are prepared to open 1NT with a singleton king or ace. West leads the ♠K, which you duck. West continues with the ♠Q, East has followed with the ♠9, ♠4, high-low discouraging. |

♠ A 6 5
♡ K
♢ K 5 3 2
♣ K 9 7 6 5

Plan your play.
*Solution opposite.*

*Checklist*

**Count Tricks:** South has five tricks. Four more are needed.

**Count HCP:** North has 11, South has 13. Total: 24. Of the 16 missing, neither opponent will have 12+ (failure to open).

**Analyse the lead:** The ♠K looks like top from a K-Q-J sequence.

**Third-hand play:** East has shown no desire for spades.

**Consider the bidding:** Not applicable, except that both West and East did not open.

**Hatch your plan:** Success in diamonds might produce two more tricks, but you need four more. The club suit offers chances for four tricks. If you decide to tackle the clubs, how would you play them?

This was Board 2 of the Japan-USA final in the 2008 World Seniors' Teams.

Dealer West : North-South vulnerable

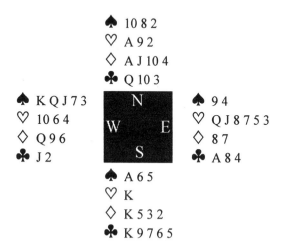

♠ 10 8 2
♡ A 9 2
◇ A J 10 4
♣ Q 10 3

♠ K Q J 7 3
♡ 10 6 4
◇ Q 9 6
♣ J 2

♠ 9 4
♡ Q J 8 7 5 3
◇ 8 7
♣ A 8 4

♠ A 6 5
♡ K
◇ K 5 3 2
♣ K 9 7 6 5

The East-West methods did not allow either to open and the Japan South chose a weak 1NT opening despite the singleton heart. West led the ♠K, ducked, followed by the ♠Q, which South won.

As West was the presumed danger hand with the spade length, South continued with a low club to the ten. If West had the ♣A, West would always come in, but it was important not to let West in with, say, ♣J-x-x. East won and had no spade to return.

South won the heart exit and cashed the club winners, pitching a heart and a spade from dummy. As East was the safe hand, declarer continued with the ◇K and a diamond to the jack. That worked, too, and declarer finished with eleven tricks for +660.

At the other table the Japan East-West played in 3♡ for –100. The contracts in other finals were 5♣ South +600, 2♡ –50 (Open) and 3♡ –150, 3NT North –300 (Women's).

**14.** Dealer South : East-West vulnerable

| ♠ Q 10 | West | North | East | South |
|---|---|---|---|---|
| ♡ 2 | | | | 1NT (1) |
| ◇ 7 5 4 3 | Pass | 3NT | All pass | |
| ♣ A Q 10 9 6 2 | (1) 15-17 | | | |

With a long suit as a source of tricks, players are prepared to gamble on 3NT.

West leads the ♡K. If you duck, West will continue with the ♡Q and ♡J, East following. East plays ♡7 – ♡4, high-low discouraging. Plan your play.

| ♠ A 5 2 |
| ♡ A 8 3 |
| ◇ A Q 10 9 2 |
| ♣ J 7 |

*Solution opposite.*

*Checklist*

**Count Tricks:** South has four tricks. Five are needed.

**Count HCP:** North has 8, South has 15. Total: 23. There is no evidence of the location of the other 17 points except that West appears to hold 6 points in hearts.

**Analyse the lead:** The ♡K looks like top from a K-Q-J sequence. East would encourage hearts with the ♡J.

**Third-hand play:** East has shown no interest in hearts.

**Consider the bidding:** Not applicable.

**Hatch your plan:** The club suit provides an opportunity for the five tricks you need. Suppose you lead the ♣J and it wins. Can you see a danger if you take a second finesse? Would you be prepared to take that risk?

This was Board 28 of the Japan-USA final in the 2008 World Seniors' Teams.

Dealer South : East-West vulnerable

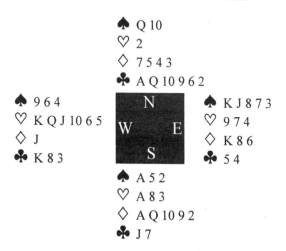

&spades; Q 10
&hearts; 2
&diams; 7 5 4 3
&clubs; A Q 10 9 6 2

&spades; 9 6 4
&hearts; K Q J 10 6 5
&diams; J
&clubs; K 8 3

&spades; K J 8 7 3
&hearts; 9 7 4
&diams; K 8 6
&clubs; 5 4

&spades; A 5 2
&hearts; A 8 3
&diams; A Q 10 9 2
&clubs; J 7

West led the &hearts;K against 3NT. It is a hard decision whether to hold off or not, because a spade switch could be dangerous. In practice defenders rarely know to switch to your danger suit and so holding off in hearts is sensible. What next?

You have four tricks on top. Your best hope is that the &clubs;K is onside. You lead the &clubs;J at trick 2: three – two – four. If you repeat the club finesse, all is well and you make 3NT easily.

The Japan South feared East might be holding off with the &clubs;K. To finesse again and lose would kill dummy. South elected to play the &clubs;7 to the ace. Then came a diamond to the queen, the &diams;A and a third diamond. East was down to spades only and led the &spades;J. South ducked in hand and had made nine tricks the hard way. At the other table North-South played in 3&clubs; and made twelve tricks.

In the other finals the results were 5&clubs; North +420, 5&diams; South +400 (Open) and 3NT South +400, 4&clubs; South +190 (Womens).

**15.** Dealer South : East-West vulnerable

|  | West | North | East | South |
|---|---|---|---|---|
| ♠ K 6 5 2 |  |  |  | Pass |
| ♡ Q | 1♣ (1) | 1♢ | Pass | 2NT |
| ♢ A Q 8 3 | Pass | 3NT | All pass |  |
| ♣ K 7 6 5 | (1) 3+ clubs (playing 5-card majors) |  |  |  |

West leads the ♡2 (fourth-highest). Dummy's
queen wins. You play the ♣5: three – queen –
nine, followed by the ♢4: two – queen – five
and the ♣6: two – jack – ace. West returns the
♣8, taken by the king. East plays the ♣10.

♠ Q 8 3

♡ K 10 7 5          Plan your play.

♢ K 7 4

♣ Q J 4            *Solution opposite .*

*Checklist*

**Count Tricks:** After trick 5, South has seven tricks (one heart,
three diamonds and three clubs after the 3-3 split).

**Count HCP:** North has 14, South has 11. Total: 25. Most of the
missing points, including the three aces will be with West.

**Analyse the lead:** The ♡2 will be from a 4-card suit headed by
the ace. It is possible but unlikely that West began with ♡A-x-2.

**Third-hand play:** East played high-low in clubs, reverse count.

**Consider the bidding:** West opened the bidding and East passed.
Almost all of the missing strength will be with West.

**Hatch your plan:** An extra trick might come from a 3-3 split in
diamonds and you can set up a spade trick. What is West's likely
hand pattern? How do you make the most of your chances?

Board 3, Round 5, of the 2008 World Teams Championships:

Dealer South : East-West vulnerable

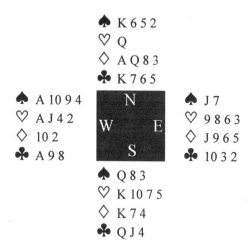

♠ K 6 5 2
♡ Q
♢ A Q 8 3
♣ K 7 6 5

♠ A 10 9 4
♡ A J 4 2
♢ 10 2
♣ A 9 8

♠ J 7
♡ 9 8 6 3
♢ J 9 6 5
♣ 10 3 2

♠ Q 8 3
♡ K 10 7 5
♢ K 7 4
♣ Q J 4

South is in 3NT after West opened 1♣, playing 5-card majors. After the missing clubs turn out to be 3-3, South had seven tricks. As West turned up with exactly three clubs and has led the ♡2, West figures to have a 3-4-3-3 or 4-4-2-3 pattern. All will be well if diamonds are 3-3, but what if West's pattern is 4-4-2-3?

Cash the thirteenth club, everyone discarding a heart, and the ♢K and the ♢A. Diamonds are not 3-3. You are now safe whether West throws the ♡J or a spade. Play a low spade: seven – eight – nine. No matter how West wriggles, West can make only the two major aces from here.

Results: Open Teams: 32 North-South pairs bid 3NT and 22 made it. Women's: 29 were in 3NT and 22 were successful. Seniors: 14 pairs played 3NT and 9 made it. That means 22/75 failed in 3NT.

**16.** Dealer West : North-South vulnerable

|       | West | North | East | South |
|-------|------|-------|------|-------|
| ♠ 7 6 | Pass | 2◊ (1) | Pass | 2NT (2) |
| ♡ 8 4 2 | Pass | 3♣ (3) | Pass | 3NT |
| ◊ K J 10 6 5 4 | Pass | Pass | Pass | |
| ♣ A 8 | | | | |

(1) Weak two in diamonds  (2) Strong inquiry

(3) Maximum and a top honour in clubs

```
      N
  W       E
      S
```

West leads the ♣2 (fourth-highest).

♠ K Q J 9   Plan your play. If you duck in dummy, East
♡ A 10 9 5  wins and returns a club. What now?
◊ A 7 3 2
♣ J         *Solution opposite.*

*Checklist*

**Count Tricks:** South has four tricks.

**Count HCP:** North has 8, South has 15. Total: 23. There is no indication where the missing points lie.

**Analyse the lead:** The ♣2 is almost certainly from a 4-card suit and that means East began with six clubs.

**Third-hand play:** If you take the first club, East will no doubt encourage a club continuation.

**Consider the bidding:** Not relevant, but West is a passed hand.

**Hatch your plan:** How should you play the diamonds? Assuming you can pick up six diamond tricks, your tally will be eight tricks. How can you hope for one more?

This is from the European Open Teams, 2008.

Dealer West : North-South vulnerable

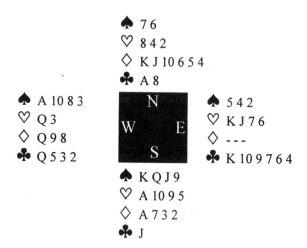

Although North had shown a high card in clubs, West began with the ♣2, fourth-highest, against 3NT. On any lead but a club South would have an easy time as long as South starts the diamonds with the ◇A.

Some might take the ♣A and try to sneak a spade at once. That is not likely to succeed. A slightly better hope is that West has led from a club suit headed by the K-Q and so you duck in dummy. East takes the ♣K and returns a club. There is no chance now that an opponent will duck if you try to sneak a spade trick.

As in many instances, it pays to run your long suit. Although the defence might seem obvious, even talented players err in discarding. As East had greater club length, declarer played West to have the ◇Q. After the ◇A, he finessed the ◇J and ran the diamonds. On the first four East threw two spades and two hearts and West the ♠8. On the fifth diamond East shed a club and West the ♠3. South had let a spade and a heart go. When East threw a club (??) on the sixth diamond, it was all over. South played a spade and had nine tricks.

**17.** Dealer East : Nil vulnerable

| | | | |
|---|---|---|---|
| ♠ K Q | West | North | East | South |
| ♡ K 10 4 | | | 2◇ (1) | 2NT |
| ◇ 7 5 2 | Pass | 3NT | All pass | |
| ♣ Q J 7 3 2 | (1) 6-10 points, six hearts or six spades | | | |

West leads the ◇Q: two – king – four. East returns the ◇9, taken by the ace. When you cash the ♠K, ♠Q, West plays ♠2, ♠3 and East the ♠4, ♠J. East-West play reverse count.

♠ A 9 8 6
♡ A J 6        Plan your play.
◇ A 8 4
♣ A 9 5        *Solution opposite.*

*Checklist*

**Count Tricks:** South has seven winners. Two more are needed.

**Count HCP:** North has 11, South has 17. Total: 28. East has turned up with 4 HCP (◇K, ♠J) of the 6-10 for the 2◇ opening.

**Analyse the lead:** The ◇Q is top of a Q-J-10 sequence.

**Third-hand play:** East's play of the ◇K, followed by the ◇9 shows a doubleton diamond, confirming West's holding. The East-West spade plays are inconsistent. One is not giving true count.

**Consider the bidding:** If East does have a 6-card major, it must be in hearts.

**Hatch your plan:** If East has six hearts, you can easily collect another trick from the hearts. You can also take a club finesse, but if it loses West will have three diamonds to cash. How do you intend to proceed? Can you manage if West has the ♣K?

This is from the European Open Teams, 2008.

Dealer East : Nil vulnerable

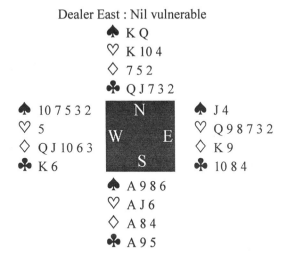

♠ K Q
♡ K 10 4
◇ 7 5 2
♣ Q J 7 3 2

♠ 10 7 5 3 2
♡ 5
◇ Q J 10 6 3
♣ K 6

♠ J 4
♡ Q 9 8 7 3 2
◇ K 9
♣ 10 8 4

♠ A 9 8 6
♡ A J 6
◇ A 8 4
♣ A 9 5

South has seven tricks. The natural place to look for the extra tricks is in clubs, but if you lose a club to West, three more diamonds will lay you low. Test the spades first. When both opponents follow to two rounds of spades, East's 6-card suit must be hearts. Hence you cash the ♡K and finesse the ♡J, followed by the ♡A. That gives you one extra trick and you need only one more. On the hearts West discarded a spade and a diamond. What now?

You can discover the spade layout by cashing the ♠A. When East shows out, you know West began with five spades, one heart, five diamonds and two clubs. Having let a spade and a diamond go, West is down to one spade, two diamonds and two clubs.

You exit with a spade. West can cash two diamonds, but must then lead a club to give you your ninth trick. Had West discarded the ♣6, you would have had to cash the ♣A and hope the ♣K dropped.

**18.** Dealer West : Both vulnerable

♠ J 10 9 5
♡ 8 6 5 3
◇ 9 6
♣ A 6 4

| West | North | East | South |
|------|-------|------|-------|
| Pass | Pass | Pass | 1◇ |
| 1♡ | Dble | Pass | 2♡ (1) |
| Pass | 2♠ | Pass | 2NT |
| Pass | 3NT | All pass | |

(1) Very strong hand

```
      N
  W       E
      S
```

♠ 6 2
♡ A K Q 2
◇ A K 8 5 2
♣ K 3

West leads the ♡4.
Which heart do you play from dummy?

Plan your play after dummy's heart wins.

*Solution opposite.*

*Checklist*

**Count Tricks:** South has seven winners. After dummy's heart wins trick 1, you are up to eight.

**Count HCP:** North has 5, South has 19. Total: 24. West is a passed hand, but overcalled on a jack-high suit. West is likely to have about 8-10 more points.

**Analyse the lead:** For the overcall, West should have all five missing hearts. The ♡4 is a strange choice rather than the ♡J.

**Third-hand play:** Not applicable.

**Consider the bidding:** West's overcall is based on a very weak suit and so West will have reasonable outside strength.

**Hatch your plan:** The opponents can take three spade tricks at will. If dummy has won trick 1, the best chance for your ninth trick is from the diamonds? How will you play the diamonds?

This arose in the European Open Teams, 2008.

Dealer West : Both vulnerable

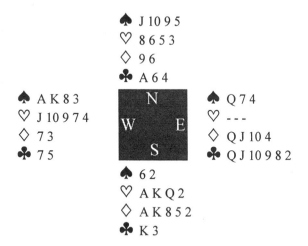

&spades; J 10 9 5
&hearts; 8 6 5 3
&diams; 9 6
&clubs; A 6 4

&spades; A K 8 3
&hearts; J 10 9 7 4
&diams; 7 3
&clubs; 7 5

&spades; Q 7 4
&hearts; - - -
&diams; Q J 10 4
&clubs; Q J 10 9 8 2

&spades; 6 2
&hearts; A K Q 2
&diams; A K 8 5 2
&clubs; K 3

West's fatuous 1&hearts; overcall led to 3NT by South and kept North-South out of the doomed 4&hearts;, reached at the other table.

Hoping partner held a heart honour, West began with the &hearts;4 rather than the normal &hearts;J. Naturally you cover in dummy and avoid the mechanical &hearts;3. You started with seven tricks and the extra heart trick brings you to eight. Where will you find the other trick needed?

You lack the entries to set up a spade trick and so you look to the diamonds for your ninth trick. How should you play the diamonds?

Start with the &diams;9 from dummy, not the &diams;6. This caters for West holding &diams;7 singleton and also for the existing layout. East actually played low on the &diams;9, which won. Diamonds were cleared and when East did not switch to a spade, South made ten tricks. If East did cover the &diams;9, South wins, crosses to the &clubs;A and plays the &diams;6. If East ducks, play the &diams;8. If East covers, you win. When the &diams;7 drops, your &diams;8-5-2 is worth two tricks against East's &diams;Q-4.

**19.** Dealer East : Both vulnerable

| ♠ 9 4 | | West | North | East | South |
|---|---|---|---|---|---|
| ♡ 9 6 2 | | | | Pass | 1NT |
| ◇ Q 5 4 3 2 | | Pass | Pass | Pass | |
| ♣ J 10 5 | | | | | |

West leads the ♠3 (fourth-highest).
East plays the ♠J.

Plan your play.

| ♠ A 5 | If you duck, East will return a spade. |
|---|---|
| ♡ A 10 7 3 | |
| ◇ A K 10 6 | *Solution opposite .* |
| ♣ Q 9 2 | |

*Checklist*

**Count Tricks:** South has five winners. Two more are needed.

**Count HCP:** North has 3, South has 17. Total: 20. The location of the missing points is unknown.

**Analyse the lead:** The ♠3 can be from a 4-card or a 5-card suit.

**Third-hand play:** The ♠J denies the ♠10, but can be from a 4-card or 5-card holding headed by the Q-J or K-Q-J. It will not be headed by the jack only. That would mean West's suit was headed by the K-Q-10 and then the ♠K would be led.

**Consider the bidding:** Not relevant, except East is a passed hand.

**Hatch your plan:** As long as diamonds are not 4-0, two extra tricks are available there. What is the problem in the diamond suit?

This comes from a national teams event in 2008:

Dealer East : Both vulnerable

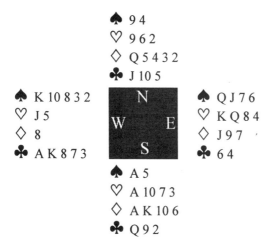

```
              ♠ 9 4
              ♡ 9 6 2
              ◇ Q 5 4 3 2
              ♣ J 10 5
♠ K 10 8 3 2      N        ♠ Q J 7 6
♡ J 5                      ♡ K Q 8 4
◇ 8          W       E     ◇ J 9 7
♣ A K 8 7 3      S         ♣ 6 4
              ♠ A 5
              ♡ A 10 7 3
              ◇ A K 10 6
              ♣ Q 9 2
```

West's pass over 1NT was very timid, but that is what happened. Most East-West pairs played in spades, nine in a part-score and three in 4♠, all making.

South has five top tricks. Two more are available if diamonds are 2-2 or 3-1. There is one hitch. If diamonds are 3-1, the diamond suit will block on the fourth round because of dummy's weak spot cards.

Noting the opening lead, the ♠3, as fourth-highest, South knew the spades would be 5-4. As the defence could not take more than six tricks, declarer returned the ♠5 at trick 2. East won, eyed the position suspiciously, but then played a third spade. South threw the ◇10 and the diamonds were no longer blocked. South actually made an overtrick when West switched to a low club after the spades. To defeat 1NT the defence need to retain communication in spades and switch to hearts after South exited with a spade.

**20.** Dealer North : Nil vulnerable

♠ 3
♡ Q 5 3
♢ 10 7 4 2
♣ Q J 8 7 2

| West | North | East | South |
|------|-------|------|-------|
|      | Pass  | 1♠   | Double |
| Pass | 2♣    | 2♠   | 2NT   |
| Pass | 3NT   | All pass | |

West leads the ♠7: three – jack – nine and East returns the ♠K. You take the ♠A and West plays the ♠6.

♠ A 10 9
♡ A 2
♢ A 6 5 3
♣ A K 9 6

Plan your play.

*Solution opposite.*

*Checklist*

**Count Tricks:** South has eight winners. You need one more.

**Count HCP:** North has 5, South has 19. Total: 24. East will have almost all of the missing high cards for opening bid and rebid.

**Analyse the lead:** The ♠7 followed by the ♠6 shows a doubleton.

**Third-hand play:** The ♠J followed by the ♠K indicates that East's spades are headed by the K-Q-J.

**Consider the bidding:** East's bidding has shown at least six spades and as West began with a doubleton, you place East with seven spades, plus a pretty decent hand for taking a second bid opposite a passed hand.

**Hatch your plan:** Given that East has almost all the missing strength, can you see any hope for a ninth trick?

This comes from the final of a State Open Teams in 2008.

Dealer North : Nil vulnerable

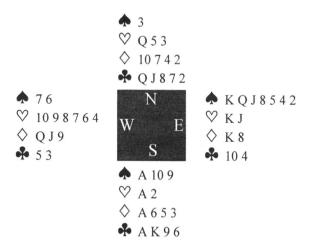

```
                    ♠ 3
                    ♡ Q 5 3
                    ◇ 10 7 4 2
                    ♣ Q J 8 7 2
  ♠ 7 6                              ♠ K Q J 8 5 4 2
  ♡ 10 9 8 7 6 4        N            ♡ K J
  ◇ Q J 9           W       E        ◇ K 8
  ♣ 5 3                 S            ♣ 10 4
                    ♠ A 10 9
                    ♡ A 2
                    ◇ A 6 5 3
                    ♣ A K 9 6
```

The bidding and early play showed that East had started with seven spades and a strong hand. East thus figured to hold both red kings. A slight hope for South is that East's ♡K is bare.

Running your long suit first in the hope of a discarding error is often a good idea. South ran five rounds of clubs and East threw three spades. That convinced South that East had started with a 7-2-2-2 pattern. If 7-1-3-2, East could have let a diamond go.

When South continued with a low diamond from dummy, East played low and that was curtains. South took the ◇A and returned a diamond. East won and could cash two more spades, but then he was left with ♡K-J and had to give the last two tricks to declarer. East could have discarded the ◇K on the clubs or risen with the ◇K on the first round of diamonds. Either would have saved the day. On the bidding South was likely to have the ♡A and so the impending endplay should have been foreseen.

**21.** Dealer East : Both vulnerable

♠ 9 7 5 3
♡ Q 10
♢ A 10 5 4 3 2
♣ K

| | West | North | East | South |
|---|---|---|---|---|
| | | | 1♣ | 1NT |
| | Pass | 2♣ (1) | Pass | 2♡ |
| | Pass | 3NT | All pass | |

(1) Stayman

West leads the ♠6, fourth-highest. East wins with the ♠A and switches to the ♣4: 3 – 9 - K.

♠ K 10
♡ K 5 4 3
♢ K 7
♣ A Q 8 5 3

Plan your play.

*Solution opposite.*

*Checklist*

**Count Tricks:** After trick 1 South has six tricks.

**Count HCP:** North has 9, South has 15. Total: 24. East will have most of the missing high cards for the 1♣ opening.

**Analyse the lead:** Apply the Rule of 11 to the fourth-highest ♠6, there are five cards higher than the six with North, East and South. You have four and East's ♠K was the fifth. West's spades will be headed by the queen-jack.

**Third-hand play:** East's ♣4 aims to knock out your entry to the diamonds, but also suggests East began with only one or two spades.

**Consider the bidding:** Already noted above.

**Hatch your plan:** You need three more tricks, but even if the diamonds are 3-2, how can you reach dummy to use them?

Board 26 from the final of the 2008 World Women's Teams:

Dealer East : Both vulnerable

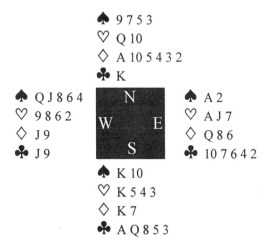

♠ 9 7 5 3
♡ Q 10
◇ A 10 5 4 3 2
♣ K

♠ Q J 8 6 4
♡ 9 8 6 2
◇ J 9
♣ J 9

♠ A 2
♡ A J 7
◇ Q 8 6
♣ 10 7 6 4 2

♠ K 10
♡ K 5 4 3
◇ K 7
♣ A Q 8 5 3

West led the ♠6 (fourth-highest) against 3NT at both tables and East won with the ♠A. China's East returned a spade. South played three rounds of diamonds and had no troubles: +630.

England's East returned the ♣4, knocking out dummy's entry to the diamonds. Declarer played three rounds of diamonds. East won and switched back to spades. South won, cashed the ♣A and exited with a low club. East won and returned a club. The defence scored two heart tricks later for one down.

As the ♠6 lead, fourth-highest, marks West with the ♠Q, ♠J (Rule of 11), East must have almost all of the other missing HCP. Play a diamond to the king, cash the ♠K and the ♣A, play a diamond to the ace and then give East the lead in diamonds. A heart return allows you to reach dummy. If East plays a club, finesse the ♣8, cash the ♣Q and put East back on lead with the fifth club. East can take one trick in each suit, but no more.

**22.** Dealer South : North-South vulnerable

|  | West | North | East | South |
|---|---|---|---|---|
| ♠ 10 |  |  |  | 1♣ |
| ♡ J 9 8 7 | 1♠ | Dble (1) | Pass | 1NT |
| ◇ A 10 9 8 6 2 | 2♠ | 3◇ | Pass | 3NT |
| ♣ K 4 | Pass | Pass | Dble | All pass |

(1) Shows hearts

♠ A K 5 2
♡ 10 5
◇ K 7 5
♣ Q 9 7 2

West leads the ♡A and the ♡2 to East's ♡Q. East cashes the ♡K and plays the ♡3 to the ♡J in dummy. You and West throw spades. You play the ◇2: jack – king – three, and the ◇7: West follows with the ◇4.

Your move?

*Solution opposite.*

*Checklist*

**Count Tricks:** After trick 3 South has five tricks.

**Count HCP:** North has 8, South has 12. Total: 20. West bid twice and should have most of the points, but East's double will also be based on some values.

**Analyse the lead:** West started with hearts as North-South denied a heart fit and East's penalty double suggested strength there.

**Third-hand play:** East began with five hearts and has set up the fifth heart.

**Consider the bidding:** West clearly has long spades, but East chose to set up the hearts rather than shift to a spade.

**Hatch your plan:** When West follows low to the second diamond, you have a straightforward decision, finesse or play for the drop. If you make the right decision you have enough tricks for 3NT.

This comes from the World Youth Teams, 2008:

Dealer South : North-South vulnerable

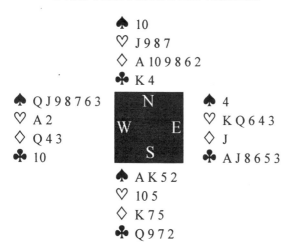

                  ♠ 10
                  ♡ J 9 8 7
                  ◇ A 10 9 8 6 2
                  ♣ K 4

♠ Q J 9 8 7 6 3            ♠ 4
♡ A 2                     ♡ K Q 6 4 3
◇ Q 4 3                  ◇ J
♣ 10                     ♣ A J 8 6 5 3

                  ♠ A K 5 2
                  ♡ 10 5
                  ◇ K 7 5
                  ♣ Q 9 7 2

The Rule of Restricted Choice recommends playing East for the ◇J bare, but there are other clues pointing in the same direction. East has strength, but did not support spades even though West showed at least six. That gives East a likely singleton in spades. Where is East's double of 3NT without the ♣A? Would East double with ♡K-Q, ◇Q-J and ♣J at best? That is hardly likely. In addition, East set up the fifth heart and figures to have an entry. That must be the ♣A. East's ♡3, the lowest heart, on the fourth round of hearts is another clue as a suit-preference signal for the lowest suit, clubs, hence the ♣A.

Once you credit East with the ♣A as well as the K-Q in hearts, how can you justify West's bidding without the ◇Q? With seven spades and the ♡A, but no more, West would surely have jumped to 3♠ at once over 1♣. You should place the ◇Q with West. That is what declarer did and finessed the ◇10 for +750.

**23.** Dealer West : Both vulnerable

| ♠ A Q 10 9 | West | North | East | South |
| ♡ 4 3 | Pass | Pass | Pass | 1NT |
| ◇ K J 6 2 | Pass | 2♣ | Pass | 2◇ (1) |
| ♣ J 10 3 | Pass | 3NT | All pass | |

(1) No major

West leads the ♡7 (fourth): three – queen – two and East returns the ♡5.

♠ 6 5 3
♡ A 2              Plan your play.
◇ A Q 4
♣ A K 7 4 2       *Solution opposite.*

*Checklist*

**Count Tricks:** South has eight tricks. Only one more is needed.

**Count HCP:** North has 11, South has 17. Total: 28.

**Analyse the lead:** West's lead is fourth-highest.

**Third-hand play:** East's return of the ♡5, the lowest heart, shows an original holding of two or four. If two, West would have started with K-J-10-9-x-x-x, a pre-empt, and would have led the ♡J. It looks as though West began with five hearts, East with four.

**Consider the bidding:** Both opponents passed, but there is no other indication where the missing points will be.

**Hatch your plan:** You need only one trick. That can come from the clubs or from the spades. How do you play to give yourself the best chance?

This arose in the finals of a national multi-teams event in 2008:

**23.** Dealer West : Both vulnerable

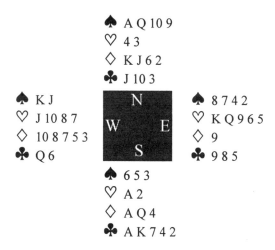

        ♠ A Q 10 9
        ♡ 4 3
        ◇ K J 6 2
        ♣ J 10 3

♠ K J                    ♠ 8 7 4 2
♡ J 10 8 7               ♡ K Q 9 6 5
◇ 10 8 7 5 3             ◇ 9
♣ Q 6                    ♣ 9 8 5

        ♠ 6 5 3
        ♡ A 2
        ◇ A Q 4
        ♣ A K 7 4 2

The ♡7 was an odd lead. Most would lead the jack from J-10-8-7.

South has eight tricks. The ninth can come from a spade finesse or from a club finesse. You can improve your chances in clubs by cashing a top club first to cater for a singleton queen with West, then cross to dummy with a diamond and run the ♣J.

One declarer minimised the chances by taking the second heart, playing a diamond to the king and running the ♣J at once. That was a speedy one down.

The club finesse is a 50% chance and so is the spade finesse. If you take one or the other it is a pure guess which to take. You can improve your chances. Cash the ♣A and the ♣K. If the ♣Q does not fall, finesse the ♠Q. You make nine tricks if the ♣Q is singleton or doubleton or the ♠K is onside. This improves your odds to about 65% and makes overtricks when the ♣Q does fall.

**24.** Dealer North : Both vulnerable

♠ J 8 7 5
♡ K J
♢ 7 5
♣ K 10 7 5 4

| West | North | East | South |
|------|-------|------|-------|
|      | Pass  | Pass | 1♢    |
| Pass | 1♠    | Pass | 2NT   |
| Pass | 3NT   | All pass |   |

N
W   E
S

♠ K Q
♡ A 4 2
♢ A K 10 3
♣ Q J 8 3

West leads the ♡10: jack – queen – two.
East returns the ♡5: four – six – king. The ♣4
is led: nine – queen – six, followed by the ♣J,
two – five – ♠6. East-West play reverse count.
Plan your play.

*Solution opposite.*

*Checklist*

**Count Tricks:** After trick 4 South has six tricks.

**Count HCP:** North has 8, South has 19. Total: 27.

**Analyse the lead:** West's ♡10 lead is top of a sequence, but the length of West's holding is not known.

**Third-hand play:** East's return of the ♡5 is consistent with an original holding of ♡Q-5-3 or ♡Q-8-7-5-3. It is normal to return the higher of two remaining cards or fourth-highest from an initial holding of four or five.

**Consider the bidding:** None relevant, but East is a passed hand.

**Hatch your plan:** You can set up enough tricks to make 3NT, but is there any danger? Should you continue clubs or set up a spade trick or two first?

This arose in the final of a national teams event in 2008:

Dealer North : Both vulnerable

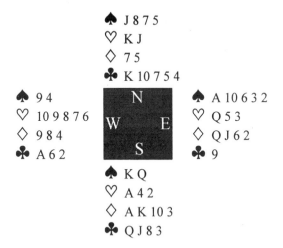

```
                    ♠ J 8 7 5
                    ♡ K J
                    ◇ 7 5
                    ♣ K 10 7 5 4
  ♠ 9 4               N           ♠ A 10 6 3 2
  ♡ 10 9 8 7 6                    ♡ Q 5 3
  ◇ 9 8 4        W        E       ◇ Q J 6 2
  ♣ A 6 2             S           ♣ 9
                    ♠ K Q
                    ♡ A 4 2
                    ◇ A K 10 3
                    ♣ Q J 8 3
```

At the table declarer shifted to the ♠K. East took the ♠A and played another heart. South won, but when the next club was played, West won and cashed two more hearts for one down.

South said that he could not tell whether the hearts were as in the diagram or whether West had started with 10-9-6 and East with Q-8-7-5-3. There are some clues. South needs to ask why West has ducked the clubs twice.

If East had the long hearts, West would take the ♣A earlier, certainly when South played the ♣J at trick 4. If East's ♣9 was reverse count from three, West would know South started with only two. West's failure to take the ♣A earlier indicated that West needed it as the entry to the hearts.

At the other table the play in 3NT began the same way, but South continued with the third round of clubs. It was easier there as East had opened with a weak multi-2♠.

**25.** Dealer West : East-West vulnerable

| ♠ A K 9 8 5 | West | North | East | South |
|---|---|---|---|---|
| ♡ A J 9 7 4 | 1♢ | Double | Pass | 2♣ |
| ♢ J 5 | Pass | 2♢ | Pass | 2NT |
| ♣ A | Pass | 3♢ | Pass | 3NT (end) |

You might not like the bidding, but that is how it went. 2♢ was strong and 3♢ begged South to choose a major. West leads the ♠10.

♠ Q
♡ 8 2          Plan your play.
♢ A 10 7 3
♣ Q J 10 8 7 2          *Solution opposite.*

*Checklist*

**Count Tricks:** South has six tricks.

**Count HCP:** North has 17, South has 9. Total: 26. Most of the missing strength will be with West for the 1♢ opening.

**Analyse the lead:** West's ♠10 appears to be top from a doubleton, perhaps a singleton.

**Third-hand play:** Not applicable.

**Consider the bidding:** West opened 1♢, but chose a short suit lead. West clearly has no good suit to lead.

**Hatch your plan:** You have a source of tricks in clubs, but after the spade lead, your entries do not permit you to unblock the ♣A, knock out the ♣K and return to the club winners. Where can you hope to collect three more tricks?

This arose in the final of a national teams event in 2008:

Dealer West : East-West vulnerable

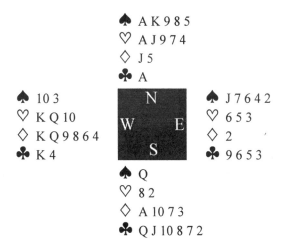

♠ A K 9 8 5
♡ A J 9 7 4
◇ J 5
♣ A

♠ 10 3
♡ K Q 10
◇ K Q 9 8 6 4
♣ K 4

♠ J 7 6 4 2
♡ 6 5 3
◇ 2
♣ 9 6 5 3

♠ Q
♡ 8 2
◇ A 10 7 3
♣ Q J 10 8 7 2

You lack the entries to set up the clubs. You can build up an extra trick in spades, but one trick is not enough. Your best bet for the three extra tricks is from the heart suit. You and dummy have 26 HCP. The ♠10 lead places the ♠J with East. The bulk of the other 13 points will be with West, who opened 1◇. Your best chance is to find West with both top honours in hearts.

 Lead the ♡8 at trick 2. If West were to follow with a low heart (not in this case), the odds are reasonable to play the ♡J rather than run the ♡8. On the actual layout, if West plays the ♡10, you have it easy. West will probably play the ♡Q or ♡K. You can survive if you take it, but you can also duck in dummy and let West find an exit.

In practice, South ducked West's ♡Q and West exited with the ♣4 to dummy's ♣A. Now South can play the ◇5 to the ◇A and finesse the ♡J. You make four hearts, three spades and two aces.

**26.** Dealer East : Nil vulnerable

|  | West | North | East | South |
|---|---|---|---|---|
| ♠ A 9 6 2 |  |  | Pass | 1♣ |
| ♡ A K 7 6 | Pass | 1♡ | Double | Rdble (1) |
| ◇ 9 8 | 2◇ | 3◇ (2) | Double | 3♡ |
| ♣ A 8 6 | Pass | 3♠ | Pass | 3NT (end) |

(1) Shows three hearts exactly (2) Strong hand

West leads the ◇2 (thirds-and-fifths): eight – king – seven. East returns the ◇4, taken by the ◇A, West ◇5. South leads the ♡J: Q – K – 5, followed by the ♠A: seven – four – five and the ♠2: king – three – ♣5. East exits with the ◇3: queen – six – ♠6.

Plan your play. *Solution opposite.*

♠ Q 8 4 3
♡ J 10 8
◇ A Q 7
♣ Q J 10

*Checklist*

**Count Tricks:** After trick 5, South has eight tricks (two spades, three hearts, two diamonds and the ♣A).

**Count HCP:** North has 15, South has 12. Total: 27. East will have about 9-11 for the takeout double by a passed hand.

**Analyse the lead:** Playing thirds-and-fifths, West's ◇2 will be from three cards or five. The diamonds are either 3-5 or 5-3.

**Third-hand play:** East's ◇4 return is consistent with ◇K-4-3 or ◇K-x-x-4-3. East's later play of the ◇3 can in theory still be from K-J-10-4-3 initially or from K-4-3.

**Consider the bidding:** East's first double should show spades and diamonds. East's second double asks for a diamond lead.

**Hatch your plan:** One option for the extra trick is the club finesse. Can you do any better?

This comes from the final of the 2008 Vanderbilt Teams (USA):

Dealer East : Nil vulnerable

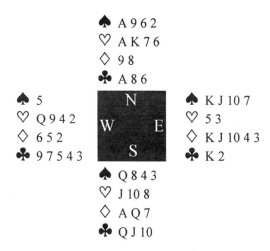

&spades; A 9 6 2
&hearts; A K 7 6
&diams; 9 8
&clubs; A 8 6

&spades; 5
&hearts; Q 9 4 2
&diams; 6 5 2
&clubs; 9 7 5 4 3

&spades; K J 10 7
&hearts; 5 3
&diams; K J 10 4 3
&clubs; K 2

&spades; Q 8 4 3
&hearts; J 10 8
&diams; A Q 7
&clubs; Q J 10

South should judge that East has five diamonds. East's takeout double implies 4+ diamonds and the double of 3◇ makes it almost certain that East is the one with five diamonds. Another clue is the choice of the ◇2 lead. As East has shown diamonds, West would start with the ◇J from ◇J-10-6-5-2

South judged that East had ♠K-J-10-x and ◇K-J-10-x-x and so placed the ♣K with West, else East might have opened. South ran the ♣10. East won and cashed two more diamonds for one down.

If East did start with 4 spades – 5 diamonds, there is no rush to take the club finesse. South should cash the ♡10 and play a heart to dummy. What can East do? Unable to let a spade go from ♠J-10, East will throw a diamond or a club. In each case South can afford to continue with the ♣A and another club. If West has the ♣K, South is all right, as there is no entry to East's diamonds.

**27.** Dealer West : North-South vulnerable

♠ A 8 7 3
♡ A J 9 8 7
◇ 5
♣ A Q 8

North opened 1♡ and South revealed a limit raise in hearts. After North made a game try, South bid 3NT, passed out. No E-W bidding.

West leads the ♠2, fourth-highest, ducked to East's ♠K. East switches to the ◇3.

Plan your play.

*Solution opposite .*

♠ Q 6 5
♡ Q 4 3
◇ A Q 10 4
♣ 7 4 2

*Checklist*

**Count Tricks:** After trick 1, South has five tricks (two spades and an ace in each of the other suits).

**Count HCP:** North has 15, South has 10. Total: 25. West as a passed hand will not have more than 11 HCP.

**Analyse the lead:** West's ♠2 as fourth-highest means the spades are 4-2 or possibly 3-3. West could have three or four spades, but the 4-card spade holding is likely.

**Third-hand play:** East's switch to the ◇3, a low card, suggests interest in diamonds.

**Consider the bidding:** Not applicable.

**Hatch your plan:** The obvious place for extra tricks is the heart suit. Even if you score four tricks from the hearts, you still have only eight in all. What is your plan for the ninth trick?

This comes from the final of the 2007 Transnational Open Teams.

Dealer West : North-South vulnerable

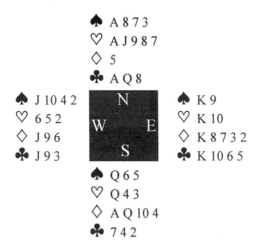

♠ A 8 7 3
♡ A J 9 8 7
◇ 5
♣ A Q 8

♠ J 10 4 2
♡ 6 5 2
◇ J 9 6
♣ J 9 3

♠ K 9
♡ K 10
◇ K 8 7 3 2
♣ K 10 6 5

♠ Q 6 5
♡ Q 4 3
◇ A Q 10 4
♣ 7 4 2

After East wins with the ♠K, South has five tricks. The best source for more tricks is from the hearts. If they divide 3-2, you have three extra tricks there. East's switch to a low diamond indicates interest in the suit led. That makes it likely that East has the ◇K and South should play the ◇Q. If the ◇Q loses to the king, West is very likely to return a diamond, giving you two tricks there after all. When the ◇Q wins, play a low heart to the jack. If that wins, continued with a low heart to the queen. As the cards lie, East takes the ♡J and, with hearts 3-2, South now has an easy nine tricks.

At the table, South played the ◇A on East's ◇3. He ran the ♡Q to East's king and East played another low diamond. South put in the ◇10, losing to the jack. When West switched to a club, declarer could not avoid losing five tricks. South had two chances to do the right thing in diamonds and East's switch to the ◇3 should have been a big clue.

**28.** Dealer South : North-South vulnerable

♠ 10
♡ K Q 6
◇ K J 7 6
♣ 9 7 6 4 2

| West | North | East | South |
|------|-------|------|-------|
|      |       |      | 1NT (1) |
| Pass | Pass | Pass |       |

(1) 12-14

♠ K 9 8 5
♡ J 9
◇ A 9 5 3
♣ A J 5

West leads the ♡5, thirds-and-fifths, and dummy's ♡K is taken by the ace. East returns the ♡3: jack – two - six.

Plan your play.

*Solution opposite.*

*Checklist*

**Count Tricks:** After trick 1, South has five tricks (two hearts, two diamonds and one club).

**Count HCP:** North has 9, South has 13. Total: 22. Neither opponent has a very powerful hand (failure to double).

**Analyse the lead:** West's ♡5, followed by the ♡2 at trick 2 here, indicates a 4-card suit when playing thirds-and-fifths. With six hearts, West would have led the ♡4, then played the ♡2.

**Third-hand play:** East's ♡3 return, the lowest heart as West played the ♡2, shows an original holding of two or four, in this case four.

**Consider the bidding:** Not applicable.

**Hatch your plan:** You need two more tricks. Should you aim to find them from the diamonds or the clubs?

This arose in a semi-final of a national teams event in 2007:

Dealer South : North-South vulnerable

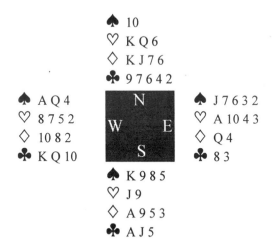

After East's heart return at trick 2, South has five tricks. Should South go after diamonds or clubs?

A successful finesse of the ◇J and a 3-2 diamond break gives you two extra tricks. If clubs are 3-2, you also have the two tricks needed. Which chance is better?

Firstly, a 3-2 break at 68% is better than a 50% chance. Secondly, you can try both as long as you try the clubs first. If the ◇J finesse loses, East can shift to a spade, low, queen, and a heart return from West leaves you with only six tricks.

At trick 3, play the ♣A and a second club. They can knock out the ♡Q, but another club gives you seven tricks safely. If clubs are 4-1, you have time to finesse the ◇J later. The opponents cannot take three spade tricks quickly on any spade layout.

**29.** Dealer North : East-West vulnerable

|  | West | North | East | South |
|---|---|---|---|---|
| ♠ A K 6 3 2 |  | Pass | Pass | 1♣ |
| ♡ K 5 | 1NT (1) | Double | 2♣ (2) | Double |
| ◇ 7 6 4 | 2◇ | 2♠ | Pass | 3♣ |
| ♣ 9 4 2 | Pass | 3◇ (3) | Pass | 3NT (end) |

N
W    E
S

(1) 4-major, long minor    (2) Pass or correct

(3) Asking for a diamond stopper

♠ 10
♡ 9 8 6 2
◇ K Q 9
♣ A Q J 10 5

West leads the ◇5, 4th-highest, to East's ◇J.

Plan your play.

*Solution opposite.*

*Checklist*

**Count Tricks:** Before trick 1, South has three tricks (two spades and the ♣A).

**Count HCP:** North has 10, South has 12. Total: 22. West should have a decent hand for the intervention at this vulnerability. East has shown no signs of strength.

**Analyse the lead:** Apply the Rule of 11 to West's ◇5 lead, fourth-highest: You and dummy have five cards higher than the ◇5 and East has just played the only other higher card. West has clearly led from ◇A-10-8-5-x(-x).

**Third-hand play:** Nothing relevant.

**Consider the bidding:** Based on West's two-suited 1NT overcall, West will have 5+ diamonds plus four hearts or four spades.

**Hatch your plan:** Which path will you take to find nine tricks?

This arose in the final of the 2008 Asian Cup Open Teams:

Dealer North : East-West vulnerable

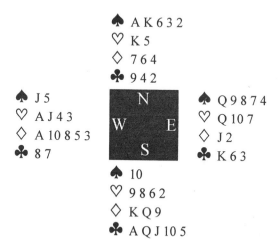

♠ A K 6 3 2
♡ K 5
♢ 7 6 4
♣ 9 4 2

♠ J 5
♡ A J 4 3
♢ A 10 8 5 3
♣ 8 7

♠ Q 9 8 7 4
♡ Q 10 7
♢ J 2
♣ K 6 3

♠ 10
♡ 9 8 6 2
♢ K Q 9
♣ A Q J 10 5

West led the ♢5 against 3NT and East played the ♢J. South's first decision is whether to win this or duck. South has two spade tricks and has to hope for five club tricks. South will need one heart trick and so must place the ♡A with West. In that case, ducking the diamond will work only if West began with six diamonds. Taking the first diamond is fine as long as the ♡A is with West, whether West has five diamonds or six.

South won the first diamond, played the ♠10 to the ace and ran the ♣9. The club finesse was repeated and the ♣A dropped the ♣K. South cashed the other club winners and led a heart. With the ♡A well-placed, South had a heart trick and access to the ♠K. If West shows out on the second club, declarer leads a heart. South can cash the ♠A and repeat the club finesse later if West has the ♡A.

3NT was reached in two other finals and succeeded each time.

**30.** Dealer West : North-South vulnerable

| ♠ A 10 7 4 2 | West | North | East | South |
|---|---|---|---|---|
| ♡ 9 8 | 3♡ | Pass | Pass | 3NT |
| ◇ 5 4 3 | Pass | Pass | Pass | |
| ♣ Q 10 4 | | | | |

```
      N
 W         E
      S
```

♠ J 8 5
♡ K 4 2
◇ A K Q 7
♣ K 6 5

West leads the ♡Q: eight – three . . .

Plan your play.

*Solution opposite .*

*Checklist*

**Count Tricks:** You have four tricks, five if you take the ♡K.

**Count HCP:** North has 6, South has 16. Total: 22. West is not likely to have much outside of the values in hearts.

**Analyse the lead:** If West has seven hearts for the 3♡ opening, West will have started with ♡A-Q-J-10-7-6-5. Possibly West has only six hearts, but they will still be headed by the A-Q-J. With ♡A-x, East would have played the ♡A and returned a heart.

**Third-hand play:** Only relevance: East will not have the ♡A.

**Consider the bidding:** Already considered above.

**Hatch your plan:** If West started with six hearts, you are doomed whether you take the ♡K or not. East is sure to gain the lead at some point. If West started with seven hearts, you might as well take the ♡K, otherwise you might never score it. What next?

The bidding was identical at both tables in the final of national teams event in 2007 and both Wests led the ♡Q, taken by the ♡K.

Dealer West : North-South vulnerable

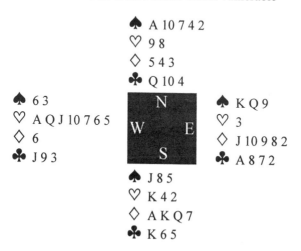

Judging West would have very little outside hearts, one South ran the ♠8 to East's ♠9. South won the ◇J switch and ran the ♠J to East, who returned the ◇10. South won and cashed three spades, discarding hearts. East came down to ◇9-8, ♣A-8-7. Declarer led the ♣4: seven – king, followed by the ◇Q and another diamond. East won, but had to give the last trick to dummy. Declarer's play was well-judged, as he would have succeeded even if East's last three clubs were ♣A-J-x.

At the other table South slipped at trick 2 by cashing the ◇A for no good reason. In Australia this is known as going on walk-about. It looked innocuous, but proved fatal. When East won the first spade, back came the ◇J. After another spade to East, the ◇10 set up two diamond tricks with the ♣A as entry and South was one down.

**31.** Dealer West : Both vulnerable

♠ K 8
♡ A 3
♢ K J 10 8 5
♣ K Q 8 3

| West | North | East | South |
|------|-------|------|-------|
| Pass | 1♢ | 1♡ | 1NT |
| Pass | 3NT | All pass | |

West leads the ♡5.

Plan your play.

♠ 10 7 2
♡ Q 6 2
♢ Q 4 3
♣ A 7 4 2

*Solution opposite.*

*Checklist*

**Count Tricks:** You have four tricks, five if the clubs are 3-2.

**Count HCP:** North has 16, South has 8. Total: 24. East should have a decent hand for the vulnerable overcall opposite a passed partner.

**Analyse the lead:** West is leading partner's suit. The ♡5 could be a singleton, top from a doubleton, middle-up-down or bottom from three to an honour. As East overcalled, West is unlikely to have more than three hearts.

**Third-hand play:** Not applicable.

**Consider the bidding:** For the 1♡ overcall vulnerable opposite a passed hand, East should have strong hearts and a good hand.

**Hatch your plan:** Clearly you intend to set up the diamonds for four more tricks. The extra trick can come from the hearts or a 3-2 club break. Is there any precaution you need to take?

This arose in the Round of 16 in the 2008 World Open Teams:

Dealer West : Both vulnerable

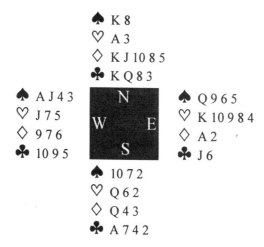

There are plenty of tricks for South. What is the problem?

If you duck the heart lead in dummy, all will be well if East wins and returns a heart. From your 1NT response, a competent defender can deduce not only that you have the ♡Q, but also that you do not have four spades. After taking the ♡K, East is very likely to switch to a spade. Now the defence can collect three spades, one heart and one diamond before you have nine tricks.

The solution is not difficult. As East was so likely to have the ♡K for the 1♡ overcall, South took the ♡A at trick 1 and played diamonds at once. As the ◇A was with East (also highly probable), 3NT was safe.

**32.** Dealer South : East-West vulnerable

|  | West | North | East | South |
|---|---|---|---|---|
| ♠ A Q 9 7 2 |  |  |  | 1♦ |
| ♡ A J | Pass | 1♠ | Pass | 1NT |
| ♢ J 10 6 5 | Pass | 2♣ (1) | Pass | 2♦ |
| ♣ K 4 | Pass | 3NT (2) | All pass |  |

(1) Forces opener to bid 2♦.

(2) Shows game values and five spades

```
      N
  W       E
      S
```

♠ 10 5
♡ 9 5 2
♢ A 8 7 4
♣ A Q J 2

West leads the ♡4, jack, king, and East returns the ♡3. East-West lead fourth-highest.

Plan your play.

*Solution opposite.*

*Checklist*

**Count Tricks:** You have seven tricks.

**Count HCP:** North has 15, South has 11. Total: 26. The location of the missing points is not known.

**Analyse the lead:** After East's return of the ♡3, West's ♡4 lead was the lowest heart and so West cannot have more than four hearts.

**Third-hand play:** East's ♡3 return, the lowest heart, indicates an original holding of two or four hearts and so the hearts figure to be 4-4. East's ♡K at trick 1 places the ♡Q with West.

**Consider the bidding:** Not applicable.

**Hatch your plan:** With hearts 4-4, you will lose three hearts at most. Which suit offers you the best prospect of two extra tricks?

This was Board 2, Round 11, 2008 World Open Teams:

Dealer South : East-West vulnerable

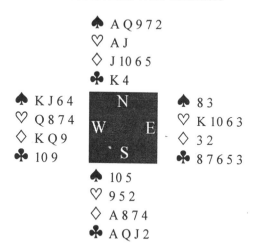

♠ A Q 9 7 2
♡ A J
♢ J 10 6 5
♣ K 4

♠ K J 6 4
♡ Q 8 7 4
♢ K Q 9
♣ 10 9

♠ 8 3
♡ K 10 6 3
♢ 3 2
♣ 8 7 6 5 3

♠ 10 5
♡ 9 5 2
♢ A 8 7 4
♣ A Q J 2

South's chance for two more tricks in spades by taking two finesses is better than tackling the diamonds. If you can score three extra spade tricks, you can risk sacrificing one in clubs. One declarer played the ♣4 to the queen and led the ♠10. West played low and the ♠10 won. The next spade went to dummy's ♠9. Declarer cashed the ♠A, ♣K, crossed to the ♢A and had nine tricks.

After the same auction and first two tricks, another declarer played ♣K, club to hand and the ♠10, king, ace. The ♢J lost to West, who played a low heart to East's ♡10 and won the heart return. When West exited with a spade, South could have succeeded by inserting the ♠9. Instead he rose with the ♠Q and came to the ♢A. When the missing honour did not drop, South was one off. South might also have succeeded after taking the ♠A by crossing to the ♢A and cashing the clubs to give West discarding difficulties.

3NT was reached 57 times in the Open Teams and succeeded 39 times; in the Women's Teams, 25/46 declarers made 3NT.

**33.** Dealer South : North-South vulnerable

| | |
|---|---|
| ♠ A J | |
| ♡ K 4 3 2 | |
| ♢ 7 6 3 | |
| ♣ A 10 9 4 | |

| West | North | East | South |
|---|---|---|---|
| | | | 1NT (1) |
| Pass | 3NT | All pass | |

(1) 11-14 points

♠ K Q 4
♡ 10 6
♢ K Q 10
♣ K 8 6 5 3

West leads the ♡7: two – jack – six and East returns the ♡Q. West takes the ♡A and continues with the ♡8, taken by the ♡K. East discards the ♠8 (high-discouraging).

Plan your play.

*Solution opposite.*

*Checklist*

**Count Tricks:** After trick 2 South has six tricks.

**Count HCP:** North has 12, South has 13. Total: 25. The location of the missing points is not known.

**Analyse the lead:** The heart situation is known. West led the ♡7 (fourth-highest) from an initial holding of A-9-8-7-5.

**Third-hand play:** Normal. East discouraged with the ♠8 discard.

**Consider the bidding:** Not applicable.

**Hatch your plan:** Have you considered the meaning behind West's ♡8 at trick 3? Your best hope for extra tricks is from the club suit. There will be no problem if they are 2-2. What if the clubs are 3-1?

The deal comes from Round 8, 2008 Under-21 World Teams:

Dealer South : North-South vulnerable

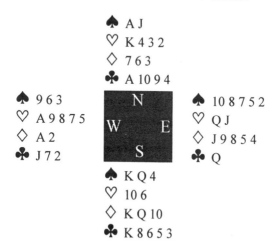

♠ A J
♡ K 4 3 2
◇ 7 6 3
♣ A 10 9 4

♠ 9 6 3
♡ A 9 8 7 5
◇ A 2
♣ J 7 2

♠ 10 8 7 5 2
♡ Q J
◇ J 9 8 5 4
♣ Q

♠ K Q 4
♡ 10 6
◇ K Q 10
♣ K 8 6 5 3

You might prefer 2♣ Stayman on the North cards, but 1NT : 3NT was the actual auction.

Since West has shown up with five hearts to East's two, there is some basis for playing West to be the one short in clubs. That is what declarer did. After taking the ♡K, South played the ♣A and another club. There was no recovery and South went two down.

The key is that West with the heart winners is the danger hand. After discarding the ◇10 on the ♡K, South should play to keep West off lead if possible. Play the ♣4 to the ♣K and after East has dropped the ♣Q, finesse the ♣10. That lands 3NT as the cards lie. If East won the second club, you must hope East also has the ◇A.

West's ♡8 at trick 3, the second-highest heart, is a suit-preference clue that West has the ◇A. In addition, if West has a singleton club, the ◇A, five hearts to the ace and a second suit, West might have competed over the 1NT opening, especially at this vulnerability.

**34.** Dealer West : North-South vulnerable

| ♠ K 5 2 | West | North | East | South |
|---------|------|-------|------|-------|
| ♡ 9 8 7 6 | Pass | Pass | Pass | 1NT (1) |
| ♢ Q 7 3 | Pass | 3NT | All pass | |
| ♣ A J 2 | (1) 15-17 | | | |

West leads the ♢4 (fourth-highest). Which diamond do you play from dummy? East will play the ♢6 regardless.

| ♠ A Q 9 | |
|---------|--|
| ♡ A J 4 | Plan your play. |
| ♢ A J 10 9 | |
| ♣ 10 6 3 | *Solution opposite.* |

*Checklist*

**Count Tricks:** After trick 1 South has seven tricks.

**Count HCP:** North has 10, South 16. Total: 26. The location of the missing points is unknown, but neither opponent opened the bidding.

**Analyse the lead:** As fourth-highest the ♢4 can be from a 4-card or 5-card suit. Rule of 11: you and dummy have six cards higher than the ♢4 and East's ♢6 is the only other higher card. If the ♢4 is fourth-highest, West has led from ♢K-8-5-4(-x).

**Third-hand play:** Nothing relevant.

**Consider the bidding:** Not applicable.

**Hatch your plan:** You can create one more trick from the diamonds, but that still leaves you one trick short. What is the best hope for that extra trick?

The deal comes from Round 8, 2008 Under-21 World Teams:

Dealer West : North-South vulnerable

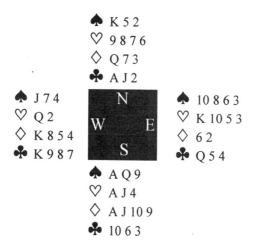

```
                    ♠ K 5 2
                    ♡ 9 8 7 6
                    ◇ Q 7 3
                    ♣ A J 2
      ♠ J 7 4          N          ♠ 10 8 6 3
      ♡ Q 2                       ♡ K 10 5 3
      ◇ K 8 5 4   W       E       ◇ 6 2
      ♣ K 9 8 7       S           ♣ Q 5 4
                    ♠ A Q 9
                    ♡ A J 4
                    ◇ A J 10 9
                    ♣ 10 6 3
```

West leads the ◇4 against 3NT. You should play the ◇Q. East will surely cover if holding the king. When the ◇Q wins and East plays the ◇6 (high-hate), South can deduce the diamond layout.

Hearts offer a better chance for extra tricks than clubs and so you lead a heart from dummy and let it run if East plays low. You hope to find East with a holding headed by Q-10 or K-10.

If East plays low, you also play low and West wins. If West shifts to a club, duck in dummy. East wins, but cannot afford a club return. East is likely to play a diamond. You play low and West wins. The rest is easy for an overtrick.

If West wins the first heart and shifts to a spade, best, take the ♠K and finesse the ♡J. When that wins, play ◇A and another diamond and you have three spades, two hearts, three diamonds and a club.

**35.** Dealer North : Both vulnerable

| | West | North | East | South |
|---|---|---|---|---|
| ♠ Q 10 4 3 2 | | 1♠ | Pass | 2◇ |
| ♡ K 9 6 | Pass | 2♠ | Pass | 2NT |
| ◇ 2 | Pass | 3♣ | Pass | 3NT (end) |
| ♣ A K 8 6 | | | | |

♠ 7
♡ A Q 8 5
◇ Q J 9 6 3
♣ Q 10 7

West leads the ♡J. You win with the ♡A and play the ♡5 to the ♡9, which wins. East has played ♡4 – ♡2, discouraging. When you play the ◇2, East wins with the ◇K and returns the ♡3.

Plan your play.

*Solution opposite.*

*Checklist*

**Count Tricks:** You have four heart tricks and three clubs.

**Count HCP:** North has 12, South has 11. Total: 23. You cannot tell how the missing points are divided.

**Analyse the lead:** The lead of the ♡J lacking the ♡9 and ♡8 suggests a lead from J-10-x. This is confirmed by the subsequent play in hearts.

**Third-hand play:** East has discouraged hearts and has played a third heart anyway, as neither black suit seemed attractive. East's play of the ◇K makes it likely that East has the ◇A, too.

**Consider the bidding:** Not applicable.

**Hatch your plan:** You can set up a diamond trick and will need to produce four tricks from the clubs. How do you proceed?

This was Board 23, Round 4, 2008 World Open Teams:

Dealer North : Both vulnerable

♠ Q 10 4 3 2
♡ K 9 6
♢ 2
♣ A K 8 6

♠ A K 9
♡ J 10 7
♢ 10 7 5 4
♣ J 5 2

♠ J 8 6 5
♡ 4 3 2
♢ A K 8
♣ 9 4 3

♠ 7
♡ A Q 8 5
♢ Q J 9 6 3
♣ Q 10 7

Although some lead the jack from J-10-x-x, most do so only from J-10-9-x or J-10-8-x and lead low from weaker holdings headed by the J-10. When declarer led the ♢2, East might have done better to duck. South might well have chosen to finesse the ♢9.

When East took the ♢K and returned the ♡3, South won in dummy, finessed the ♣10 and finished two down.

Declarer could have won the third round of hearts in hand and played the thirteenth heart. That would force a discard and might lessen the danger in spades. South can then set up a diamond trick and with clubs behaving, declarer would have nine tricks.

When East takes the ♢A (or the ♢K earlier), East can test South with a low spade return. West wins and returns the ♠9, putting declarer to the guess.

3NT was made 10/21 times in the Open, 4/13 in the Women's and 6/10 in the Seniors.

**36.** Dealer South : North-South vulnerable

♠ 6 5 4
♡ K 10 4
♢ Q 10 8 5
♣ K Q 10

♠ A J 3
♡ A Q 8 5 3
♢ K 9 2
♣ J 8

| West | North | East | South |
|------|-------|------|-------|
|      |       |      | 1NT (1) |
| Pass | 3NT   | All pass | |

(1) 15-17

West leads the ♡7: four – jack – queen. You play the ♣8 to the king and ace. East shifts to the ♠2, jack, queen, and West returns the ♠10, East plays the ♠8 and South ducks. West continues with the ♠7 to East's ♠K, which you take. All follow when you play the ♡3 to the king. What next?

Plan your play. *Solution opposite.*

*Checklist*

**Count Tricks:** You have eight tricks.

**Count HCP:** North has 10, South has 15. Total: 25. There are no clues where the missing points lie.

**Analyse the lead:** The ♡7 turned out to be a short suit lead. Initially it might have been top from a doubleton or second-highest from three or four low cards.

**Third-hand play:** East's shift to the ♠2 shows interest in spades. East's ♠K on the third round of spades could be from an original holding of three or four spades. West's play of the ♠Q, then ♠10, then ♠7 could be from Q-10-7 or Q-10-9-7.

**Consider the bidding:** Not applicable.

**Hatch your plan:** Where is your ninth trick?

This was Board 15, Round 7, 2008 World Open Teams:

Dealer South : North-South vulnerable

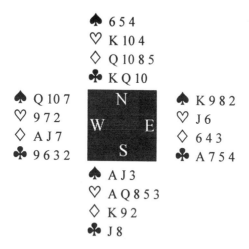

♠ 6 5 4
♡ K 10 4
◇ Q 10 8 5
♣ K Q 10

♠ Q 10 7
♡ 9 7 2
◇ A J 7
♣ 9 6 3 2

♠ K 9 8 2
♡ J 6
◇ 6 4 3
♣ A 7 5 4

♠ A J 3
♡ A Q 8 5 3
◇ K 9 2
♣ J 8

It is fascinating how even top players have lapses of concentration. At trick 7, South was in dummy with the ♡K and had eight tricks.

You have to accept that if the player with the ◇A has the last spade you are doomed, no matter how you play. After taking the ♡K, South should either play the ◇Q or a diamond to the king. As the cards lie, all is well. You have entries to both hands.

How did South go wrong? After the ♡K South cashed the ♡10. Now the only entry to hand was the ♣J, but to use that would leave the ♣Q marooned in dummy. Trying to recover, South played the ◇Q, which held, followed by the ◇5 to the ◇9. West collected two diamond tricks for one down.

Moral: You need to maintain focus at all times.

3NT was made 30/46 times in the Open, 23/29 in the Women's and 19/20 in the Seniors.

**37.** Dealer East : Nil vulnerable

|  | West | North | East | South |
|---|---|---|---|---|
| ♠ Q 4 |  |  | Pass | 1NT (1) |
| ♡ A 8 4 | 2♣ (2) | 3NT | All pass | |
| ◇ Q 10 9 4 3 | (1) 15-17 | | | |
| ♣ Q 8 3 | (2) Both majors | | | |

West leads the ♡K: four – five – six,
followed by the ♡Q, taken by the ace. East
discards the ♠10 (high-hate).

♠ A K 7
♡ J 6 2          Plan your play.
◇ K 7 2
♣ A J 7 5       *Solution opposite .*

*Checklist*

**Count Tricks:** After trick 2, South has six tricks.

**Count HCP:** North has 10, South has 16. Total: 26. West figures to
have most of the missing strength, particularly as West's spades are
very weak.

**Analyse the lead:** You already know that West began with six
hearts to the K-Q-10 and East began with a singleton heart. The fact
that West continued with the ♡Q, even if that was in the hope of
pinning the ♡J with South, suggests that West has outside entries.

**Third-hand play:** Nothing relevant.

**Consider the bidding:** Already noted above.

**Hatch your plan:** You need three more tricks. Which is the best
route to those tricks?

This was Board 8, quarter-finals, 2008 Under-21 World Teams:

Dealer East : Nil vulnerable

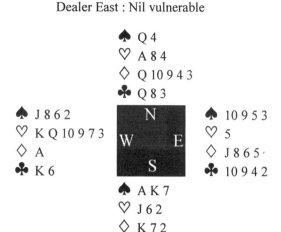

♠ Q 4
♡ A 8 4
♢ Q 10 9 4 3
♣ Q 8 3

♠ J 8 6 2
♡ K Q 10 9 7 3
♢ A
♣ K 6

♠ 10 9 5 3
♡ 5
♢ J 8 6 5
♣ 10 9 4 2

♠ A K 7
♡ J 6 2
♢ K 7 2
♣ A J 7 5

Against 3NT West led the ♡K, ducked, and continued with the ♡Q, taken by the ace. South needs three more tricks and the best source for those tricks is the diamond suit. It would be an error to take the club finesse. West wins and plays a third heart. Now even if the clubs are 3-3, you have only eight tricks. As the cards lie, you would be two down.

As West is the danger hand, you should plan to keep West off lead later. Both Souths led a diamond to the king at trick 3. West won and played a third heart to South's jack. Now declarer played a diamond. East scored the ♢J, but South had nine tricks.

On the actual layout, it works to run the ♢10 from dummy at trick 3, but this would be fatal if West had started with ♢A-J, ♢A-J-x or ♢A-J-x-x. The low diamond to the king ensures West can never gain the lead with the ♢J.

**38.** Dealer East : North-South vulnerable

|  | West | North | East | South |
|---|---|---|---|---|
| ♠ 4 3 |  |  | Pass | Pass |
| ♡ Q 2 | Pass | 1◇ | Pass | 1♡ |
| ◇ K Q 7 5 4 | Pass | 2♣ | Pass | 2NT |
| ♣ A K 10 3 | Pass | 3NT | All pass |  |

West leads the ♣6: ace – nine (high-hate) – five. The ◇4 goes to the jack and ace. West continues with the ♣8: three – seven – queen. All follow on the ◇3 to the king, but on the ◇Q, East discards the ♣2.

Plan your play.

*Solution opposite.*

♠ J 7 6 5
♡ A J 8 4
◇ J 3
♣ Q J 5

*Checklist*

**Count Tricks:** After trick 2 you have seven tricks.

**Count HCP:** North has 14, South has 10. Total: 24. There are no clues as to the missing points, except that East is a passed hand.

**Analyse the lead:** It is unusual that West has chosen a M.U.D. lead in clubs rather than the unbid suit, spades.

**Third-hand play:** East had the chance to signal on the third diamond, but discarded the ♣2 instead. That suggests that East has values in both majors.

**Consider the bidding:** Not applicable.

**Hatch your plan:** You can set up an extra diamond trick by playing a fourth diamond, but the opponents might be able to take three spades then. If you take the heart finesse and it wins, you are up to eight tricks, but no ninth. What do you decide to do?

This arose in the final of a national teams event in 2008.

Dealer East : North-South vulnerable

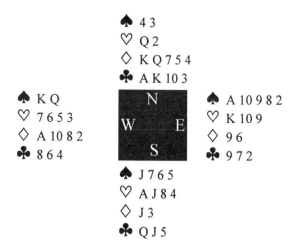

♠ 4 3
♡ Q 2
◇ K Q 7 5 4
♣ A K 10 3

♠ K Q
♡ 7 6 5 3
◇ A 10 8 2
♣ 8 6 4

♠ A 10 9 8 2
♡ K 10 9
◇ 9 6
♣ 9 7 2

♠ J 7 6 5
♡ A J 8 4
◇ J 3
♣ Q J 5

After cashing the ◇K and ◇Q and finding the 4-2 break, declarer panicked. Afraid to play a fourth diamond in case the opponents cashed spades, declarer played the ♡Q, king, ace. After a heart to the jack and the top clubs, South had no more tricks and was –100.

This was a very timid effort. You should play the fourth diamond. West has shown no inclination yet to play a spade. Maybe West will still stay off the spades. If West shifts to a heart, you are home. If West plays a club, cash your winners and take the heart finesse.

It is true that the opponents might cash the spades if you play a fourth diamond, but it is highly unlikely that they can take more than four spade tricks. By abandoning diamonds, you accept a sure –100. By playing a fourth diamond you risk –200 at worst, but give yourself the chance of +600. There will be days when the opponents cannot take three spades, as in the actual layout.

At the other table South made 3NT for +12 Imps.

**39.** Dealer East : Both vulnerable

|        | West   | North  | East     | South |
|--------|--------|--------|----------|-------|
| ♠ A    |        |        | Pass     | Pass  |
| ♡ K Q 8 | 1♠ (1) | Double | Pass     | 1NT   |
| ◇ A K Q 8 7 | Pass | 3NT    | All pass |       |
| ♣ J 10 9 5 | (1) Playing 5-card majors | | | |

|   N   |
|:-----:|
| W   E |
|   S   |

♠ Q 10 8 2
♡ J 6 3
◇ 10 6 4
♣ K 3 2

West leads the ♠4. At trick 2 you play the ♣J: ace – two – seven. East returns the ♠9, ten, jack. West cashes the ♠K and continues with the ♠7. East discards the ♡9 (dislike) and dummy has pitched the ♣5 and two hearts. You cash five diamonds. West discards three hearts, South two hearts, East a heart and a club. Plan your play. *Solution opposite*.

*Checklist*

**Count Tricks:** You have eight tricks (two spades, five diamonds and one club).

**Count HCP:** North has 19, South has 6. Total: 25. West will have the bulk of the missing points, even though West's opening was in third seat.

**Analyse the lead:** The lead was fourth-highest, but you already know that West began with ♠K-J-7-4-3.

**Third-hand play:** East rose with the ♣A to push a spade through South for partner.

**Consider the bidding:** Already noted above.

**Hatch your plan:** You have come to the critical moment. You can finesse East for the ♣Q, play the ♣K and hope the ♣Q drops or play the heart and hope to endplay West to lead away from the ♣Q. Which do you choose?

This was Board 87 of the quarter-finals of the 2007 Bermuda Bowl:

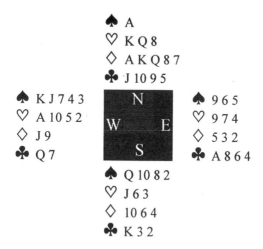

♠ A
♡ K Q 8
◇ A K Q 8 7
♣ J 10 9 5

♠ K J 7 4 3        ♠ 9 6 5
♡ A 10 5 2         ♡ 9 7 4
◇ J 9              ◇ 5 3 2
♣ Q 7              ♣ A 8 6 4

♠ Q 10 8 2
♡ J 6 3
◇ 10 6 4
♣ K 3 2

In one match the auction and early play were identical at both tables: ♠4 lead; ♣J from dummy . . . Had East played low, declarer would have to play the ♣K to succeed, an unlikely choice. Both East's rose with the ♣A to lead the ♠9 through declarer.

West captured South's ♠10, cashed the ♠K and knocked out the ♠Q. From the bidding and play, West figured to have the ♡A, else West opened with 7 HCP at most and East kept silent with two aces and three spades.

Both declarers ran the diamonds. One declarer then ran the ♣10 to West's ♣Q and went two down. The other played the ♣10 to the ♣K. The ♣Q dropped and ♣9 was declarer's ninth trick.

Why did South play that way? While West might have opened light, South felt that East would not have passed over North's double with three spades and 6 HCP. South therefore placed the ♣Q with West.

**40.** Dealer East : Nil vulnerable

|  | West | North | East | South |
|---|---|---|---|---|
| ♠ A 10 7 3 | | | 3♣ | Pass |
| ♡ A K Q 7 2 | Pass | Double | Pass | 3◇ |
| ◇ 10 4 | Pass | 3♡ | Pass | 3NT |
| ♣ A 6 | Pass | Pass | Pass | |

```
      N
  W       E
      S
```

♠ 8 5 2
♡ 8 5
◇ A J 7 5 2
♣ K 8 7

West leads the ♠K: three – six – five. The ♠4 comes next. What do you play from dummy?

Suppose you chose the ♠10. East wins with the ♠J and switches to the ◇6, two, queen. West exits with the ♠K, taken by the ace, as East discards the ♣3 (odd-encourage)

Plan your play. *Solution opposite.*

*Checklist*

**Count Tricks:** South has seven tricks.

**Count HCP:** North has 17, South has 8. Total: 25.

**Analyse the lead:** West has led the ♠K and that turned out to be from an original holding of K-Q-9-4.

**Third-hand play:** After taking the ♠J at trick 2, East switched to the ◇6, declarer's bid suit, when a club shift had to be safe.

**Consider the bidding:** East opened 3♣, yet West did not lead a club and East did not switch to a club at trick 3. Does this strike you as odd?

**Hatch your plan:** You need two more tricks and that will be easy if hearts are 3-3. You can set up an extra heart trick even if they are 4-2, but if West has the four, as is likely, you will lose three spades, one heart and a diamond. Can you see any hope for success?

This was Board 49 from the final of the 2008 World Open Teams:

Dealer East : Nil vulnerable

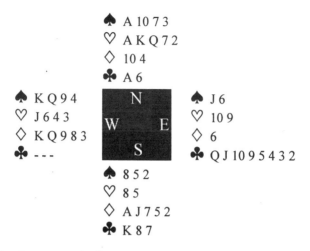

♠ A 10 7 3
♡ A K Q 7 2
♢ 10 4
♣ A 6

♠ K Q 9 4        ♠ J 6
♡ J 6 4 3        ♡ 10 9
♢ K Q 9 8 3      ♢ 6
♣ - - -          ♣ Q J 10 9 5 4 3 2

♠ 8 5 2
♡ 8 5
♢ A J 7 5 2
♣ K 8 7

After East opened 3♣, South ended in 3NT and West led the ♠K, ducked by declarer, East following with the ♠6. West continued with the ♠4.

Why did West start with a spade lead rather than a club? Only if West's spades were very strong, thought South, and so played the ♠10 on the ♠4. South figured West had started with ♠K-Q-J-4 or ♠K-Q-J-9-4 and was not about to be fooled by West's low spade.

South was jolted by East's winning with the ♠J. East shifted to the ♢6, ducked to West, who returned the ♠K. This set up the ♠9 as the fourth defensive trick. If West gained the lead in either red suit, he could cash the ♠9 to set the contract.

From West's risky choice of lead, South deduced that West must be void in clubs, otherwise that would have been the automatic choice. South cashed the ♡A and ♡K and noted with some satisfaction that East had followed with the ♡10 – ♡9. The layout was clear.

If West had no clubs, East started with eight clubs and had shown up with two spades, two hearts and a diamond. South played a club to the king and the position was confirmed. A club to the ace left this position:

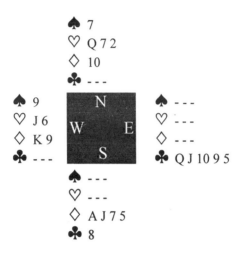

West could not afford to reduce to a singleton in either red suit, else South would just cash all the cards in that suit. In the above ending, declarer exited with dummy's ♠7. West won, but no matter which red suit West played next, declarer had the rest of the tricks. The successful declarer was Nik Sandqvist of England. Of course, South might have discovered the position earlier by playing the ♣K sooner.

*************************

If you have been diligent in following the checklist for each deal, you will hopefully have acquired the habit. You should strive to make it a life-long habit as part of your standard approach when faced with a no-trumps contract. The final deal is a good example of using the clues to come up with the right answers and produce a very elegant ending.